Community education and urban schools

Community education
and urban schools

John Boyd

Longman
London and New York

Longman Group Limited London

*Associated companies, branches and representatives
throughout the world*

*Published in the United States of America
by Longman Inc., New York*

© Longman Group Limited 1977

First published 1977

Library of Congress Cataloging in Publication Data

Boyd, John, 1935–
 Community education and urban schools.
 Bibliography: p.
 Includes index.
 1. Education, Urban—United States. 2. Community schools—United States.
 I. Title.
LC5131.B68   371.9′672′0973   77-5912
ISBN 0-582-48945-8

Set in 10pt. Times New Roman.
and printed in Great Britain by Richard Clay Ltd.

Contents

Preface

What constitutes a relevant educational experience for inner-city children? This question has been the subject of a wide-ranging debate among educationalists. Much of the earlier work dwelt on the claimed characteristics of children in urban schools, which had the effect of highlighting what was seen as their deficiencies in an educational setting. It followed that schools would need to intervene, in providing compensatory measures for children who were culturally deprived, if such children were to be equipped to compete with others in more favoured areas. The Plowden Report was the watershed in this country for the compensatory viewpoint; it also provided the basis from which a notion of community education evolved. As compensatory education has increasingly come under fire because of its claimed negative view of children as deficit systems educationally, and the value assumptions about the inner-city milieu which follow, a radical notion of community education has increasingly been advocated. The urban environment is the legitimate source of an education which is social rather than academic; through it, children will come to an awareness of the possibilities and problems of their community and will be the instigators of social change within it. A. H. Halsey's term 'constructive discontent' sums up the aims of such an education.

Alongside this radical view is developing a more moderate standpoint, in which community schools serve their locality through making their facilities available outside school hours and are focal points for community activity. But several problems need answering. Is there a community for the school to serve? The radical view has Utopian goals but are its procedures so very different from education in other areas? Is it, in fact, no more than another version of the compensatory viewpoint? And, is it bound to be so circumscribed an education that it will disadvantage children rather than equip them to become agents of social change?

Another dimension of this debate about the linked issues of equality and what counts as a relevant education can be seen in the alternative high schools in the USA. Here, the education is 'in community': the city is a huge resource for learning which is tapped by students. Although their experimental status makes them vulnerable to policy changes in boards of education, they are curriculum-focussed institutions of an arguably more radical kind than anything which has so far developed in this country.

If the community – compensatory linkage cannot be resolved, perhaps elements of both can fruitfully be included in a common education. Such an experience, if it is flexible enough to perceive and cater for important local needs, has the power to answer the questions about relevance, since it will be the means by which all children will acquire understanding of those public forms of thought which a society considers valuable enough to wish them to be perpetuated through its next generation.

Chapter 1

The role and status of compensatory education

Introduction

The designation of educational priority areas, with their focal point being the community school, has become accepted and established both by researchers and teachers as being the main answer for this country to the problems posed by education in the inner city. But, what is understood by the 'community school'? Does it provide a focal point for the community in the form of a community-based education, or is it simply a conveniently situated gathering point for shared resources and facilities for children and parents to use during their leisure time? What, for that matter, is a community? It is suggested that at this point in time, these questions remain unanswered yet educational decisions are being made as if there were clear answers. This is not surprising given the sense of crisis that urban education generates: in many areas there is more than the impression that schools do little more than contain the multitude of problems which are represented in deprived areas; that even containment is precarious, and that little by way of education can be pursued. It is the kind of setting where objective analyses can be regarded as time-wasting, or indeed a retreat from the problems on the part of interested but detached observers. Thus the kind of examination which will be seen as being appropriate will be action-orientated.

The early impetus stemmed from the Plowden Report and, in particular, the Committee's recommendations made in Chapter 5 concerning the setting up of educational priority areas. Many of the recommendations were acted upon speedily, and the notion of a community-based education received added impetus from the work and writings of such charismatic figures as Dr Eric Midwinter, the director of the Liverpool EPA project, and from Dr A. H. Halsey, the national project director.

The Plowden conception of positive discrimination, as applied to education in the inner city, can be interpreted in two broad ways. It can be viewed in terms of education being a compensatory experience, or in terms of what Midwinter and others see as an alternative and more positive response, the concept of community education. The two are clearly juxtaposed in Midwinter's thinking; they are conceptually different because they begin from different premises as to the educability of the inner-city child, and they differ in their perception of the inner-city milieu. The first sees this as drab, constricting, and the source of serious deficits in children's ability to succeed in school learning tasks, while the second sees it as vivid, dynamic, and not merely a legitimate, but the definitive focal point from which the content and style of inner-city education will develop.

Much of what is implicit in Plowden tends to favour the compensatory view. The material in Chapter 2 of the Report is illustrative; likewise the discussion in Chapter 15 of the aims of primary education, where the Committee suggests that a major aim should be that of making good the deficiencies in children's home backgrounds. Statements of this kind are central to the rationale of compensatory education. What is less clear is how the goals of programmes accepting this rationale are to be achieved in schools, given that children are seen as educational deficit systems from the beginning.

The question is raised, bearing in mind Plowden's strong influence, as to whether the community education view really is conceptually different, or is a different expression of the compensatory view. Considering both the history of failure of compensatory programmes in this country and in the USA, and the elusiveness of the community education notion, this is a crucial question. It can be approached by looking at the claimed defining characteristics of each standpoint together with their professed aims. For instance, it might be the case that the community education view represents an emotional rejection of the compensatory view, distinguished by claiming an affirmative as opposed to a negative notion of the child as learner in school.

But there are earlier influences which can be traced back to the elementary school system as it became established and developed its characteristic ethos in the late nineteenth and early twentieth centuries. The main function of the 1870 Education Act was to fill the gaps which the various voluntary religious societies had left in their provision of elementary schooling. These were mainly in the expanding industrial cities. Midwinter (1973) is illustrative about the effects which these peculiarly nineteenth-century institutions had, and still have:

> '*How much educational rope could be let out to sustain without upsetting the* status quo*? This issue haunts educational debate from the middle of the nineteenth century, through its later decades, with Forster's cry for elementary education for "masons, carpenters, joiners, and simple policemen" into our own epoch with its quarrels about secondary selection and the "more means worse" argument in terms of university entrance.*' (p. 25.)

He makes the point repeatedly, that the educational system was developed for social and economic reasons and not for the intrinsic worth of education. Again, Dearden (1968) maintains that the elementary school curriculum was dictated by one criterion – social utility. This was compounded by the institution of the device of 'payment by results' which in effect determined what was taught through what was examined. As the examination results in turn decided a school's income, there was little or no incentive to develop the curriculum beyond the 'paying subjects' which by inference fulfilled the social utility criterion.

Three further, connected factors are important here; that the curriculum was defined for the school by central government; that the progressive relaxation of the Elementary Code did not produce marked changes. The introduction to the 1904 Elementary Code represents a culmination of this liberalising movement which both sought to widen the curriculum and to extend teachers' professional freedom. Educational change began slowly to take place, but a third factor working against this was the authoritarian nature of the schools, which was so imbedded in their origins and intended function that elements of this can arguably be identified today, especially in junior schools.

An aspect of this was the unquestioning acceptance of the teacher as arbiter of knowledge. The ethos of elementary schooling is a good example of Young's (1971) proposition, that knowledge is socially and historically determined; that those in positions of power in a society will act to define what is to count as knowledge, and its accessibility to different groups. Concomitant decisions will be made about the kinds of relationships which will be permissible between those groups which are given access to knowledge, and those which make knowledge available. Young's later comments in the same essay about the contemporary educational situation agree in substance with Midwinter's and Dearden's views on elementary education, and its artefacts. What is relevant to the discussion here is Young's claim that an academic curriculum is still emphasised, with clearly demarcated, examinable subjects. This situation is underlined, he contends, by the earlier policy of the Schools Council, as a major curriculum development agency, of accepting tacitly this traditional view of the academic curriculum, by concentrating on 'low-status' areas of knowledge for pupil groups who are either academic failures in the sense that they are not participants in the public examinations structure, or are in an age-group which makes them too young to participate.

Dearden, discussing the junior school, refers to the stress placed on routine, age grouping, the marking of registers, and the exaggerated respect given to inspectors on visits. He might have referred also, as artefacts of the elementary tradition, to the continuing debate between the streamers and the unstreamers; between child-centred and teacher-directed protagonists, and the effects which secondary-school selection and transition in its different forms, even in areas which have reorganised on comprehensive lines, can and does have on school organisation, teaching approaches, pupil grouping, and the curriculum.

Midwinter claims that while society has become relatively permissive and relaxed, the school remains a basically authoritarian institution, mainly because this is the image which society retains and wishes to retain of the school. It could also be claimed that philosophers of education such as Peters (1969) have reinforced this view by arguing that in a world where the Church has lost most of its authority, only the teachers are in a position to initiate the young into the values and beliefs which a society wishes to perpetuate. Shipman (1968) also, has argued that the teacher's authority is becoming increasingly personal and charismatic in a society where values are more fluid and susceptible to change.

Much of this suggests that the formal role of teachers has not changed markedly since the beginnings of mass education. This is an important point, since the burden of this discussion is to attempt to identify links between the elementary ethos and the notion of compensatory education. The first is still recent as an actuality (the term 'elementary' was only abolished thirty years ago) and arguably is present in contemporary education, especially in secondary-modern and junior schools. There are links in the underlying assumptions of what was seen as an appropriate educational experience for the children who attended the elementary schools, and, at present, many schools in inner city areas. With elementary schools, appropriateness was measured according to the assumed and intended life chances of the mass of the population. The pressures for restraints on the breadth of the curriculum and on the duration of education were largely social and economic. The situation had much to do with an upper-middle-class ruling group prescribing what would count as a relevant education for the lower classes. This education had three intended functions: to enable them to be economically viable; to give them access to the scriptures; and to instil a measure of patriotism. The reasons for the form it took were consciously connected with maintaining a social *status quo*. At the same time, there were positive factors built into the system, socially and educationally. An educated work force would be more likely to facilitate economic expansion and change than an illiterate one; and there was the added bonus in that education would identify those gifted lower-class children who through sponsorship could be directed to higher education and entry into the professional and commercial middle classes.

But in what ways does this tradition link with the compensatory viewpoint? An examination of its organising principles and aims should help in making clear the connections.

Compensatory education

The notion of compensatory education derives from the statement that inner-city working-class children are culturally or socially deprived. Briefly, the argument is that the working-class experience of socialisation communicates and instils certain values, attitudes and perceptions which differ generally from the mainstream culture which is reflected in the way schools function. The school is a middle-class institution having a distinctive set of aims and values. The view includes the assumption that the mainstream of education is therefore determined and shaped by middle-class values and attitudes, since the middle classes are the dominant social grouping in advanced industrial societies. Working- and especially lower-working-class children will therefore be less educable than middle-class children, whose socialisation has developed attitudes and values which are part of the mainstream culture, and are therefore end-on to the cultural ethos of the school. It follows that working-class children will need an educational experience which compensates them for the differences brought about by their socialisation, and which will initiate them into the mainstream culture. Among the features of compensatory education are included an extension of nursery education which will intervene in the socialising process so that children are better equipped to accept schooling when they reach the statutory age. Also, stress is placed on language enrichment programmes which concentrate on oral language skills and reading development.

The compensatory notion of education is pervasive and is still arguably the most influential view in the context of inner-city education. It reached its fullest expression in this country in the Plowden Report, and criticism of the notion has been fairly recent (Bernstein, 1970 and Keddie, 1973, for example). The notion itself has gained more acceptance, especially from local education authorities. As the number of immigrant children entering the schools has increased, the central and organising concept of cultural deprivation has, correspondingly, been sharpened. On the other hand, Jensen's (1969) views, that some racial groups are genetically inferior and are of an inherently lower intelligence than Anglo-Saxons, for instance, suggests that the cultural deprivation–compensatory action linkage is based on false premises, so far as Negro children for example are concerned, and will fail to produce the expected increases in school achievement. Jensen makes this implication which has been contested (by Kagan, 1969, for example).

The arguments against compensatory education focus upon the notion of cultural deprivation and the assumptions which underlie it. In order to make what is being criticised more explicit, Passow and Elliott's

(1968) general conclusions from a survey of research on the characteristics of the culturally deprived will be helpful:

1. language inadequacies, including limited vocabulary and poor syntactical structure, inability to use abstract symbols and complex language forms to interpret and communicate, difficulty in developing and maintaining verbal thought sequences, restricted verbal comprehension, unfamiliarity with formal speech patterns, and greater reliance on nonverbal communication means.
2. perceptual deficiencies and problems of visual and auditory discrimination and spatial organisation.
3. a mode of expression more motorial and concrete than conceptual and idea–symbol focussed.
4. an orientation of life that seeks immediate gratification in the here-and-now rather than delaying for future advantage.
5. a poor self-image, denigrating the self's potential as person and learner.
6. aspirations and goals too modest for academic achievement.
7. apathy and detachment from formal educational goals and processes.
8. limited role behaviour skills and inadequate or inappropriate adult models.

The list as a summary of research demonstrates by inference, the criteria for a given social framework within which categories of people are appraised. But a major criticism of the concept of cultural deprivation is that the term is meaningless – everyone has a culture. In what sense then, can an individual or a group be termed 'culturally deprived'? This serves to emphasise the culture-relative point which the criticism focusses upon: that an assumption is being made that the middle-class-orientated mainstream culture is intrinsically superior to the claimed minority culture of the lower working class – whoever they are – especially in the inner city. Clearly, the assumption that the middle-class culture is in fact the mainstream can be questioned. It would appear to depend on the indices used: if they related to income and occupation exclusively, then the middle-class culture would emerge as a minority culture.

But, if the same kind of political–social indices that might be used in studying, for instance, the role and status of the elementary school in the late nineteenth and early twentieth centuries, were used as well to consider what appear to be the agreed preconditions for a successful inner city education, then it is contended that very similar conclusions could be drawn. The same kinds of perceptions, as to what characterises a suitable educational experience for a category of people are at work here. Furthermore, the assumption mentioned here earlier, that the mainstream culture and that of educational provision is determined and shaped by middle-class values, since the middle classes are the dominant political and social grouping, seems at least in the context of education and its management to be an actuality, and one with a long history behind it.

Elementary education – compensatory education

The linkage at this level between elementary education and compensatory education becomes clearer, and much follows from it which is both common and contrasting. The elementary-school child was initiated into an idea of his life chances through a narrowly conceived, authoritarian school system which professed to be a complete educational experience for all except the academically gifted for whom the 'ladder of opportunity' was provided through the scholarship system. Again, children in many inner-city schools are seen as deficit systems, who ideally need to be divested of their own culture and made over according to a middle-class mainstream conception. Implicit in this is a negative view of children from lower-working-class backgrounds. So much fundamental skills work in language development and perceptual enrichment will need to be undertaken that there will be little time for anything else: this is the natural set of consequences of a compensatory view.

Again, only those few who are able enough will really benefit within this view, through examination success and access to higher education and middle-class occupational opportunities. To compound this, the school recognises that its influence is weaker than that of the home. Schools Council Working Paper 27 '*Cross'd with Adversity*' (1970) states categorically that the home influence is four to five times greater than that of the school; so it will be an exceptionally strong-minded as well as highly intelligent lower-working-class child who will be able to break out of his constricting home environment into pastures green.

The implications are clear: that compensatory education begins with assumptions about children's academic weaknesses; this implies concentration on the sort of skills programme which in fact characterised elementary education, which will bring children 'up to standard'. This is particularly true of American practice. A well-known programme such as the Head Start Project concentrated on pre-school saturation of children in guided play, language enrichment, and cultural experiences which together were expected to build a platform for children on which they would be able to cope with the requirements of schooling on a level with their more socially favoured contemporaries. In this country the emphasis has been more on improving the physical conditions of learning and teaching, following the Plowden recommendations, and less on developing specialised programmes, though this is changing. It can be asserted that in the USA separate and specialised schemes have been evolved and more precise instruments for diagnosis and selection developed for children who are thought to be in need of compensatory help, while in this country the approach has been more general, with whole areas, and schools in areas, being designated as being eligible for special attention. Ferguson and Williams (1969) provide useful evidence for this comparison.

Thus, emphasis has been placed on reducing class sizes, providing better working conditions for pupils and staff and making available special allowances designed to attract competent teachers into the EPA schools. This perhaps represents the first phase of compensatory education here. The next is more likely to follow the American pattern by concentrating on programmes in the skills areas mentioned, and preparing teachers specifically to work in the inner city. Some evidence can be seen in the growth of local teachers' centres, the establishing of centres for urban education, and for specialised curriculum work, and a generally stronger 'applied sociology' element in teacher preparation courses.

Looking at this comparison from a different but related aspect, both elementary education and the compensatory notion regard children as being passive recipients of what the school decides to offer. They share the same view of the child as school learner. This might be claimed as a general characteristic of schooling, and it becomes a matter of degree rather than difference in treatment. In the elementary schools children were offered what was both a utility curriculum and one which it was considered would be sufficiently demanding for the lower classes. Inherent in the comments made by Forster when introducing the 1870 Bill was a view of these children as being unintelligent and not suited for an academic education, even if this was desirable. A similar view, in a more sophisticated form, is current. Pidgeon (1970) concludes from a summary of research that a large number of teachers still have a capacity view of intelligence, which assumes that literacy, numeracy, and more general educational attainments as the school measures these are the main indicators of intelligence. Since working-class children as a category tend to perform less well in school than middle-class children, the further assumption, that they are innately less intelligent than middle-class children, is easily made. Daniel and Maguire (1972) for example, quote a Stepney secondary-school headmaster who claimed that he had never met an intelligent or literate skinhead.

The fact that a small proportion of such children do succeed academically tends to prove such teachers' point, in their eyes: that there are
bound to be some intelligent working-class children.

At the same time, arguably the strongest organising principle within
the compensatory education notion was equality of educational opportunity. Researchers such as Floud, Halsey and Martin (1956), Halsey,
Floud and Anderson (1961), Douglas (1964) and Wiseman (1964) were
influential in this country in pointing out social class and environmental
factors which made for inequalities. The Plowden Committee's notion
of positive discrimination is a strong avowal of the principle of equality
as applied to schooling. That the compensatory notion evolved from
attempts to ameliorate social injustices in education is a point which
some of its critics, especially Bernstein (1970) and Keddie (1973), have neglected. What is at fault however, are the inbuilt limitations of the notion
itself, its view of education, very much in terms of schooling, as being
fixed and given; of standards to which children should be brought, and
assumptions made about the nature of social class sub-cultures in the
context of education.

Similar points can be made about the elementary school, except that
it was not ostensibly working towards equality of opportunity in the
mid-twentieth century sense. But the essential value of education was
acknowledged, and not entirely from a social utility perspective. There
were pressures quite early on, following the 1870 Act, to extend the
range of elementary education both by liberalising the Code and by
widening scholarship opportunities. And it can be claimed that elementary education created its own form of challenge for equality by being so
successful that it was forced to operate outside its laid-down terms of
reference: witness the growth of higher grade schools and 'higher tops'
in elementary schools from the 1880s, until a point was reached when
these forms of para-secondary education had to be acknowledged
formally by the central government.

Another linking factor in this discussion is the relative political
powerlessness of working-class people in inner-city areas. This has not
changed markedly even with the development of local government.
Indeed, in inner city boroughs where Labour-controlled councils are
elected term after term, it can be argued that individuals and groups have
less influence over policy, since the policy-making body tends to become
more atrophied and isolated in its working because of the lack of any
opposition threatening enough to challenge it. Coates and Silburn (1970)
have commented on the social and educational implications:

*'The social structure that generates poverty generates its own shabby
education system to serve it; and while it is useful to attack the symptom,*

the disease itself will continually find new manifestations if it is not under-
stood and remedied. The solution to poverty involves, of course, the redis-
tribution of income, but more than that, it requires the redistribution of
effective social power. Self-confidence, no less than material welfare, is a
crucial lack of the poor, and both can only be won by effective joint action.
More contentiously, it seems to us that educational provision alone cannot
solve even the problems of educational poverty, if only because in this
sphere there are no *purely educational problems.'* (p. 73.)

Mays (1962) has commented on the willingness of many inner-city
parents to hand over to schools some of the crucial problems to do with
bringing up children and of the ways in which teachers were obliged by
circumstances to take on part of a social worker role. Midwinter (1973)
has remarked on the difficulties he and his colleagues often experienced
in finding the entrance to Victorian school buildings – a characteristic
they shared with Victorian hospitals.

Two schools

At this point, two illustrations from possible practice should be helpful
in crystallising several discussion areas. If deprivation is thought to be
functionally linked to family and environmental circumstances, then
schools are likely, it is suggested, to react in two broadly defined ways.
The first of these involves imposing a 'school' set of values which conflict, perhaps consciously, with neighbourhood values where these can
be identified. It would be indicated to children that their 'home' values
must be discarded at the school gates, and that while they are in school,
they will conform to rules of behaviour which make assumptions as to
how children should behave in school. These might well be perplexing
to the extent that they engender hostility, especially if there is neither the
means nor the intention to explain the 'why' of the rules. If they are
enforced punitively, most children will accept them, but a proportion
are likely to react with aggression which in turn will invoke the appropriate punishments and perhaps a scapegoat label. The equivocal position of corporal punishment in such a setting suggests problems: it
resembles many parents' ways of getting obedience, which could well
compromise the different nature of the rules which are to be followed,
the values they encapsulate, and their assumed intrinsic superiority.

This picture, of a certain type of school, frequently a junior school,
expands when teachers' attitudes to children's potential is examined.
Generally, the view will be that a very few children will benefit from the
rigours of schooling. The majority's life chances are thought to be

limited, and organisation and teaching methods will reflect this. Such a school is likely to be streamed or use ability grouping in its classrooms, and to have a relatively narrow curriculum, or one which is a scaled-down version of a traditional secondary school curriculum. Parental attitudes may range from open antipathy – a 'them and us' view – to indifference, and to acceptance without question depending on how successful the school is with their own children, in controlling them, instilling basic skills, and getting them into secondary schools of their choice – which is also likely to be the headteacher's choice. If the school is in an area which has retained secondary school selection, the last factor will be emphasised.

This is very much a representation of the ethos of elementary schooling. A tightly organised, competitive junior school of this kind can gain respect and acceptance in a lower-working-class neighbourhood. Such a school is a known quantity in a changing world. It reflects parents' view of what schooling is by resembling the schooling they received.

The second suggested type of reaction entails the school accepting negatively what the children bring from their culture into the school. Teachers' expectations will usually be low because these children, though friendly, outgoing and likeable, are also 'dim' and innately so. They are perceived as being reluctant to learn; they have short attention spans; they are happiest working in a routine way, such as copying from books and off the blackboard, and at art and craft activities.

The school's climate may be described as 'therapeutic': there is agreement that children should be happy at school, with the assumption being made that they should not be faced with learning tasks which they might find threatening. Compared with the first school, there will be tolerance of a high noise level, moving about, and children moving from one task to another as the mood takes them. Again, there will be problems: some children will be bored and become disruptive because they are not challenged with work which is in line with their ability. Teachers' perceptions of this will not necessarily indicate that it is a plea for more demanding tasks, but as symptoms of maladjustment due to a poor quality home background. This is not to deny that there is a relatively high incidence of disturbance among children in the inner city, compared with those in more favoured areas, but in this situation, where teachers feel threatened professionally because what they offer as teachers is rejected, it can be a small step to labelling all such 'rocking the boat' behaviour as being caused by maladjustment. Parents' views of such schools are frequently derogatory: they are 'soft'; they do not represent schooling as they knew it; their children do not progress in those learning skills most easily recognised: reading and computation.

These then are impressions of school 'types' rather than full-blown models, which it is claimed are extensions of teachers' attitudes towards inner-city children, where these attitudes are essentially negative. Both would claim to be coping with an inner-city situation in that they are meeting those educational deficits brought about by home environment as they interpret these. Both could claim to be providing forms of compensatory education. Both reject the neighbourhood culture. The first is reminiscent of elementary schooling at its more repressive, but the second makes very much the same kinds of assumptions about children's potential in the short term and their life chances in the longer term.

This approach could be extended by looking at differently orientated schools, including those which make efforts to liaise with parents. The basic premise is not necessarily altered, that children and their parents are expected to accept what the school is offering, and that a sharp distinction is drawn between the teachers as professionals, who decide on goals, content, and organisation and the recipients who can be involved, if teachers so agree, in those tasks that do not entail decisions as to what is taught and how. Middle-class parents have recognised their relative statutory impotence and, characteristically, have organised articulate pressure groups often focussed on parent-teacher organisations in single schools, or on local and national bodies such as CASE, which frequently have the power to gain access to and bring pressure to bear on the decision makers.

This is in contrast to the working-class, inner-city situation as discussed earlier. The general notion of the community school, as an institution in which parents and teachers collaborate and where the professional–non-professional distinction tends to be blurred has a peculiarly middle-class flavour. Broadly, the school is seen as a focal point for the community; again, broadly, its role is to provide the means for a more articulate expression of neighbourhood needs and of values.

The community school is seen by Halsey (1972) as the major alternative to compensatory education. The discussion in the next chapter investigates this claim. More specifically, the consideration will be whether it does differ, or whether in its present form, it is a different manifestation of compensatory education. An initial point can be made: that the idea of the community school did not come from the grassroots but has been developed by researchers concerned with the regeneration of inner-city neighbourhoods. This in itself comments on the possible nature of community education as it is perceived: what kind of remedy is it?

In summary it can be claimed that there are strong similarities between elementary education and the compensatory education notion and there are apparent historical links between them which have been strengthened rather than weakened by much educational research, and in particular, research concerned with social influences on educability, and how this has been interpreted. The inbuilt limitations of both views of schooling have been considered. They are both inherent and self-contradictory. In the first place there is a shared view of the nature of education for a category of the school population, which makes assumptions about levels of achievement for most children in this category. In the second place, there is respect for the experience of education itself, though it is the product rather than the process which is respected. While the compensatory notion stems from the intention to promote equality of educational opportunity, the elementary schools stimulated pressures for equality by being so successful as to create a demand for higher levels of education than they could provide.

Chapter 2

Community-based education and compensatory education

In the first chapter, links between the elementary ethos and that of compensatory education were identified. What is argued here is that the notion of community education far from being a radical alternative to compensatory notions, represents another manifestation of the compensatory viewpoint. Therefore, the claim that it represents a new and positive approach to education in the inner city is questioned. Furthermore, the links between elementary education and compensatory education must extend to community education: the underlying values of all three are fundamentally the same.

Bearing in mind the criticisms made of compensatory approaches, the question as to what might be an appropriate education in the inner city remains to be answered. It becomes more pointed when these criticisms and objections are considered in more detail. Since, as has been argued, all three notions have at their roots principles to do with equality of opportunity, albeit at different levels of articulation, a discussion of this principle will be of help in beginning an analysis of the nature of community education.

Halsey's discussion has particular relevance; he is one of the chief protagonists of community education in this country, and has researched and written extensively on the theme of home background and social class influence on educational achievement. He suggests that there were two early interpretations, both of which are still influential. The first has to do with equality of access to education, and the second was concerned with equality of achievement. The second very much built on the preconditions suggested by the first, that if a society is able to afford opportunity of access across the social class span, then the system, if it is just, will also allow equality of educational outcomes. It was this second interpretation which informed the American compensatory programmes, and which provided the rationale for the educational priority area recommendations in the Plowden Report.

Halsey suggests another, crucial, dimension, in which providing the means of achieving equality is contrasted with stimulating a demand for equality. It raises basic questions about the nature and function of education:

'*Education for what? The debate over equality as we have summarised it – a movement from preoccupation with equality of access towards concern with equality of outcomes as between social groups – is essentially a discussion about education for whom and to do what. In planning our intervention in schools we were forced sooner or later to consider both questions and in doing so to question whether an E.P.A. programme was anything more than a new formula for fair competition in the education selection race.*

What assumptions could or should be made about the world which our E.P.A. children would enter after school? Were we concerned simply to introduce a greater measure of justice into an educational system which traditionally selected the minority for higher education and upward social mobility out of the E.P.A. district, leaving the majority to be taught, mainly by a huge hidden curriculum, a sense of their own relative incompetence and impotence – a modern, humane and even relatively enjoyed form of gentling the masses?' (p. 11.)

His answer was the idea of the community school as outlined by the Plowden Committee and adopted in various forms by the EPA research project directors. Halsey sees the community school as the social nexus for a whole range of reforms, at bottom, political, which would so change the nature of inner-city areas that the quality of life and employment opportunities would improve radically. The school's role in this design is to service change by supplying educated personnel to work within this new social milieu, and at the same time, to play a part in bringing about change by sensitising children and their parents to what is positive and distinctive about their community. This in itself raises questions – perhaps indeed it begs the question – as to what characterises a community, and whether in fact a notion of community exists in inner-city areas, given the range of physical changes alone, taking place within them.

The general aims of community education as Halsey sees it have been outlined. At face value they seem radical, almost revolutionary. What is not entirely clear, however, is whether this style of urban regeneration is conceived of as part of a given political-social structure which entails adjustments to the *status quo*, or if the structure itself is being challenged. The resolving of this central point should in turn make clear whether Halsey's proposals are at heart compensatory, following Plowden, or do in fact offer a radical interpretation of educational need. In turn, important questions are raised as to how much change is seen as being possible; what forms it will take; in what kinds of ways will political power structures in inner-city areas be changed, if at all, and to what extent will people living in these areas have more direct control over policy that affects their area? Or, alternatively, have direct access to those making and instituting policy?

Social change – educational change

Several points and implications emerge from these questions. To refer back to Halsey, there are strong reasons for asserting that he sees the kinds of change he advocates as taking place within a relatively unchanged political-social structure. For example, there is his equivocal attitude towards the scale of change as evidenced in his treatment of Popper's distinction between holistic and piecemeal reform in a society. Halsey talks about 'the appropriate scale of the piecemeal' and suggests that the debate concerns 'the level of ambitiousness of social engineering which may be required to change an undesired state of affairs'. He sees Popper's distinction as representing a continuum, therefore, rather than a dichotomy, whereas the two types of reform are distinct, since different political-ideological rationales underpin them. The first is essentially revolutionary, the second democratic.

Given Halsey's position, then, his use of value-loaded words such as 'appropriate' and 'undesired' becomes problematic: to whom, and in what sense? What does 'social engineering' mean? Is social engineering something which is conceived outside, and then imposed on a neighbourhood? This raises another question, as to the nature of the interaction which will bring about change. On the face of it, if a neighbourhood is to be transformed by creating more and varied job opportunities, improving the quality of housing and recreational facilities, improving social services and making them more accessible, and improving the quality of schooling, then outside forces in the form of change agents will be needed.

But, what counts as change in these circumstances? There is the danger that a superficial view of change will be accepted. An example of this, which has been implemented, is the Plowden Committee's assumption, that if physical conditions in schools were improved, then attitudes towards school would change as a matter of course.

What is left out is the position of the recipients. There is no necessary connection between changing physical conditions and changing attitudes. Change is something which is perceived by people; it has much to do with beliefs, assumptions, and personal and group values. Change, therefore, which is organised and initiated in a neighbourhood by agencies outside it does not carry the entailment that it will be perceived as being beneficial, an improvement on what was there before. Involvement of those living in the neighbourhood so that they cease to perceive themselves as recipients, and see themselves as agents bringing about change would seem to be a necessary condition. In summary, the need for change is something that is perceived from within a neighbourhood; change itself will in turn be initiated and controlled from within.

But this represents an ideal-type situation. What is problematic here is the relative political powerlessness of inner-city inhabitants, which both Halsey and Midwinter have commented on. In large-scale, complex operations where urban regeneration programmes are begun, there is a very real danger that change governed by what outside agencies see as being beneficial, and informed by their scale of values will be brought about. In such a situation it is hard to talk meaningfully about change in the way it has been defined here, as it is likely to be a physical pheno- menon only, and may even be seen as a devaluing of the neighbourhood by those who live in it. What sort of consultation, then, is possible, and at what levels? It is clear that interaction is necessary between the neighbourhood and the agencies, but what will this entail in respect of initiative and control?

In summary, outside agencies may well bring about the physical conditions of change but this does not of itself or necessarily modify peoples' attitudes. Yet, paradoxically, it would seem that people in the inner city are powerless to bring about change of and by themselves.

Much therefore seems to depend on the growth of neighbourhood and community awareness as a facilitator of change. In this respect, Mid- winter (1973) claims that centralised government appears to have reached its apotheosis and that there are signs of an increasing emphasis on local political control. By local control, he means some form of concerted community action. His definition of 'community' is that adopted by the Seebohm Committee: 'the existence of a network of reciprocal social relationships which among other things ensure mutual aid and give those who experience it a sense of well-being'. He suggests that the community rather than local government as it presently func- tions might interpose between the individual and the state. He claims that 'the community in this way could represent the individual validly and confront the state confidently'. The role of the state in this relation- ship would be to provide services and resources, and the community would choose from these according to its needs at any given time. Other services might be shared by smaller groupings of communities. He outlines a possible modular system with each module being served by interdisciplinary teams of officials. Allegiance would be to the module rather than to an individual professional department. He does not underrate the complexities, and the political-social upheavals intimated, and he describes the whole system as being to some extent at least, visionary.

Change and the community school

This then is the setting in which the community school would operate. Midwinter (1972b) is clear about the school's role in terms of community education, as being the means of supplying such a system with personnel who would be educated according to its organising principles and functioning.

It is at this point that questions might be raised about the possible curriculum content of the community school, if only at the level of general principles. On the face of it, given the scenario of community regeneration which Midwinter (1972b) especially has drawn, the curriculum of community education would need radically to differ from that of the mainstream of education, especially in its development of particular attitudes and perspectives in pupils in order to serve community needs as Midwinter (1972b) and Halsey see these. Indeed, curriculum aims, content, patterning and presentation represent together the major focal point, if schools are to succeed in producing the sort of community-orientated adults which they are intended to produce.

What does Midwinter (1972b) – arguably the leading protagonist in this country of the radical view of community education – have to say about the basis for such a curriculum? His main contention is that the social environment would be the curriculum focus. A community school would necessarily have a community-orientated curriculum, and this curriculum would be social rather than academic. Halsey's term 'constructive discontent' is seen as the shaping principle.

At this point some problems arise as to what characterises a 'social' curriculum compared with an 'academic' one. To begin with, it is not clear in what way the content of the social differs from that of the academic. Also, there seems to be a confusion noted in the work of some of the EPA research projects, between exploring possible procedures, and establishing coherent guiding principles for the operating of a socially orientated curriculum.

It will be useful then initially to examine the community curriculum notion in terms of Halsey's discussion in *EPA Problems and Policies*, Volume 1 of the Educational Priority series of reports. He has much to say about the Liverpool project of which Midwinter was the director. Firstly, there is the move already noted from the 'academic' to the 'social' (Halsey's quotation marks), and the drawing of resources for learning and especially for language work from the children's experience of their environment. Secondly, more time should be given over to creative work such as art and craft, drama and movement, which were shown to be important in interesting and involving parents in their children's learning. Thirdly, skills rather than information should be concentrated upon, as a means of exploring that world which is judged to be relevant to the inner-city child. Fourthly, both school climate and teaching attitudes and approaches need to be changed to bring them into line with the social orientation of the curriculum.

A central aspect of community education concerns parents – how is the role of parents perceived by the community school, and how are they to be involved? As a preliminary comment, much was made of a conclusion from the Liverpool project, that the most potentially fruitful endeavours were joint parent–children undertakings in investigating their social environment, though this was not objectively evaluated. It would seem that the form and quality of parental involvement is a major focus within the community-based curriculum, yet the following discussion suggests that this has not been sufficiently thought through.

The characteristic which all the EPA projects had in common was the implementation of a given set of strategies in a designated area. They all adopted in various interpretations the principle of the community school. It is not clear to what extent and in what sorts of ways parents were involved in decision making throughout the duration of the projects, or whether they were consulted about participation either on their own behalf or their children's, once the areas were chosen for the action research projects. That parents were involved and that this was part of the agreed plan is clear enough, notably in the Liverpool and the Deptford projects. The projects' rationale and planning were conceived by a group of professionals and put to work by the group in an area designated by central government. The point is, that both parents and children were in the role of recipient, receiving a given educational programme, as is the case in programmes of compensatory education, yet the aims and rationale of community education make the assertion that it is a positive alternative to the compensatory approach. Is the term 'community' merely being substituted for 'compensatory' and underneath it all is there the same view, of cultural deprivation at work?

Again, an extension of this role of parents, in compensatory programmes, is to provide support for the programme by allowing themselves to be involved on the programme's terms in their children's education. One example is Bereiter and Engelmann's (1966) especially rigorous project where a condition for children being included was their parents' agreement to participate. The Head Start project also tried in several ways to involve parents.

A rejoinder to this might be that given the present distribution of political power, which renders inner-city parents particularly lacking in this, no alternative measures could be possible, whether they are community-focused or compensatory by nature. This in itself draws the community notion and the compensatory notion closer to one another, but the argument falls some way short at this stage of claiming that community education is another interpretation of the compensatory viewpoint. It could be argued though that a precondition for successful community education, which would be the achievement of its long-term aims, is a period of education which is compensatory in style. Further, it could be asserted, from the evidence available, that the real fruits of community education are impossible to quantify at this point in time; that attempts to establish success or failure are meaningless, since the whole enterprise has to be seen in a time-scale covering two or three generations. 'Constructive discontent' is a slowly-acquired attitude of mind which will come to fruition when a generation has passed through the community schools, and when this is accompanied by the kinds of changes in the social distribution of political power which Midwinter predicts.

But there are problems in this sort of linkage. Compensatory pro-grammes are conceived of in terms of the educational mainstream; they are part and parcel of the educational *status quo*, while the radical inter-pretation of community education presents itself as a relevant alternative to the mainstream. Therefore, there is a basic disagreement between the aims of compensatory programmes, and those of community education. It is almost contradictory, then, to talk about a compensatory experience being a precondition for successful community education programmes, because successful compensatory measures would in practice deny the need for the sort of community education which Midwinter advocates.

At the same time, though, there is an acknowledgement of deprivation in both viewpoints. The pedagogy of compensatory education seeks to inculcate those basic skills which are necessary to educational advance, whatever interpretation of education is involved, and stems from the notion of educational disadvantage. Advocates of community education place an equally strong emphasis on basic skills as a means to achieving longer-term goals, but make the claim that the social environment, far from disadvantaging children, is the legitimate source of their educa-tional content in the fulfilling of both short- and long-term objectives.

Thus there is an uneasy, visible, juxtaposition between two apparently opposed concepts of education which hints at stronger links below the surface.

Further ambiguities emerge when the proposed role of the community school and the concept of community itself are considered. The success of radical community education depends upon fundamental changes at the political and social grassroots which Midwinter claims are already manifesting themselves. Halsey is more circumspect on this point. Also important here are complex, parallel changes alongside schooling, in the distribution and use of social resources. Halsey and Midwinter say that the community school cannot develop of and by itself, but that it will play a leading part in bringing about change. The notion of change which has been discussed here has everything to do with a conscious dissatisfaction with the *status quo* developing in a neighbourhood. It cannot be imposed, though a climate beneficial to change can be created. The context can be contrived: what happens within it and as a result of it cannot be. Whether community education as developed so far is part of a suitable strategy for creating such a context is still a further question.

Concerning this, there have been criticisms of Midwinter's claim that a grassroots movement towards change can be facilitated. Merson and Campbell (1974) are sceptical of the concept of community which they see as a myth, when applied to the inner city. They are suspicious of what they see as a translation of the notion from the Cambridgeshire village colleges setting of Morris, and also the Leicestershire community schools, to an urban setting. Also, they make much of political power-lessness as being a characteristic of an inner-city population:

'*The defining characteristic of the people living in inner cities is the fact of their political oppression – their deprivation is seen in their lack of power and access to sources of decision about their future. The real decisions over their present and future conditions are made elsewhere, in government, production, business and commerce and in the professions. Such oppressed areas may be said to exist in response to the distribution of power and rewards in the social structure. And it is from this relationship that all their other deprivations stem. Crucially, in the context of the present discussion, decisions about the provision of housing, education, and employment reside in an economic elite who exist politically, professionally socially and usually physically, outside the area, and access to this elite, and therefore to the decision-making processes, is not in the gift of the inhabitants of the oppressed area.*' (p. 44.)

Community education – compensatory education

In the light of the discussion so far, it becomes evident that the similarities between the community education viewpoint and that of compensatory education are more significant than the differences. This can be examined further by extending the discussion begun in the first chapter, of the links between the elementary ethos and compensatory education.

What elementary education and compensatory measures have in common among other features discussed here, is the similarity of the kinds of decisions made about what is to be taught, and the relationship between these decisions and the mainstream of education. If the mainstream is taken to be an education shaped predominantly by middle-class perceptions and values, with stress placed on academic prowess, then the elementary school can be seen as an institution which emphasised an aspect of this, in terms of a social utility curriculum. More fundamentally, it mirrored this mainstream and in some respects converged with it. A clear convergence point is the scholarship system which underlined the entry qualifications into middle-class education: a willingness to accept and understand its values and goals, if only for instrumental reasons. Initiation into these was through the elementary school; and not only for the scholarship successes. Robert Lowe's comment, that the elementary-school product, through his education, should be enabled to recognise a higher culture and defer to it is illuminating, though not in the way that Lowe intended.

Similarly with compensatory education programmes. The deficit notion has been discussed, along with its value assumptions. If Halsey's second type of equality, that of achievement, is the major organising principle for compensatory strategies, then there is bound to be strong emphasis placed on what are seen as basic educational weaknesses and their amelioration through the intervention of the school.

Further agreement exists in a shared though differently articulated notion of educability. In the elementary school the view was that only a minority of children from working-class backgrounds would be so intelligent as to gain from entry into an academically orientated education, while there is something of a double-think at work in compensatory programmes. On the one hand, only a few children will be identifiable as having sufficiently high ability to enable them to succeed in an academic education, while on the other, the view is that the majority are under-achievers because of environmental reasons, and that this situation will be changed for the better when the learning environment is improved by the school.

In both viewpoints there is the recognition of underprivilege and the desire to identify and promote ability.

By comparison, community education, at face value, has a maverick quality. The four conclusions mentioned, from the Liverpool EPA project seem to indicate a different educational perspective, marked in the shift from an academic to a social education. On the face of it, this seems to be a repudiation of the mainstream and an attempt to devise a curriculum and mode of operating which invests the social environment of the inner-city child with positive and relevant educational qualities. Why it is seen as an alternative, and a positive one, to the mainstream depends on the growth of an ideology in terms of which community education serves community regeneration and development: it is by nature, social, political, and educative.

However, when the curriculum principles of this view of community education are examined the radical nature of the proposal diminishes, since all that is being said is that reading, writing, and other language work should focus upon subject matter which is within the child's direct experience. The skills themselves are not discounted; all that is being said is that children should acquire them through interaction with their social environment. This is barely different in substance from claims made by child-centred educationalists, that children learn best through their interests, and that these will be found in the child's environment. The difference lies in the proposition that children will come to perceive their environment in a critical way if it is the source of their basic curriculum content.

What is proposed then is a generally child-centred philosophy of teaching and learning located in a social context. But, what is important is that the skills which are valued in the educational mainstream are equally valued in community education. How else might the new, socially aware population of the inner city perceive coherently the conditions in which they live and work, and be enabled to communicate what is needed to bring about change to those agencies which enable change to be brought about? Whether or not this crucial point is realised by community education advocates is a further question; Midwinter (1973) has said that community educators are at the same time more long-sighted and pessimistic than those concerned with compensatory education. He talks for instance about the short-term objectives of improving reading attainment, and the long-term goal of an educated population being involved in and initiating policy in an improved civic life. In this respect, Merson and Campbell's criticism of community education needs to be considered, that it will in fact disadvantage inner-city children in their developing those perceptions which will lead them to being able to influence their environment, because such an education is so narrowly conceived. The point becomes more telling when it is considered alongside Halsey's comment that 'The obvious danger here is of creating a second-class education for second-class citizens through curricula restricted to local horizons'.

This seems to go directly against the curriculum assertions made by Midwinter for example, and it needs to be seen in the context of both Halsey's and Midwinter's equivocal attitudes towards education in the inner city. They both appear to subscribe to a traditional view, that there will be a small number of academically gifted children in urban schools; also they seem to assent to the established means by which able working-class children can acquire an education which transfers them to the middle-class. Merson and Campbell have criticised Halsey on this point; it is a view of education which conflicts with his environmentalist concept of the nature of intelligence and of school attainment, as demonstrated in his earlier research connected with equality of educational opportunity (e.g., Floud, Halsey, and Martin (1956); and Halsey, Floud, and Anderson (1961). Discussing the Liverpool project's curriculum experiments, he says: 'These innovations do not seem to have led to problems of discipline or time wasting or to a decline in academic standards.' Midwinter (1972a) early in his discussion of the project comments: 'It struck us, that while obviously remembering the needs of the local boys with the latent talent to make good, our preoccupations should be with the huge majority who will live forever in the deprived area.'

To reiterate: compensatory education – along with the elementary tradition – starts with a received situation. There is the specified goal of equipping culturally deprived children so that they can compete within the mainstream of education on equal terms with culturally more favoured children. Community education, on the other hand, appears to repudiate the compensatory stance by asserting that children in the inner city need to be sensitised to the conditions of their environment so that they will be enabled by their education to make articulate and effective attempts to bring about change. But, for them to be able to achieve this goal, they will need the traditional skills of the educational mainstream, and this includes its accolades. They must acquire the skills and the perspectives to be able to compete successfully for more resources, greater local political power and influence so as to consolidate a position from which they can bargain successfully with the purveyors of resources and power, whether local, central, or in the public or private sectors of industry and commerce. They must be rather better entrepreneurs than the entrepreneurs themselves. In order to serve this purpose, a community notion of education must not only incorporate, but emphasise much of the current content of what has been described here as the mainstream of education.

The argument, then, is that the community education notion does not differ from that of compensatory education either in its content or its shorter-term aims. So far as its longer-term aims are concerned, there is no necessary entailment that children will develop a critical concern for their neighbourhood through having experienced a community-located and community-focused education. Again, the context can be established but this will not in itself lead to the development of particular perspectives, unless these become the subject matter of indoctrination, rather than an educational experience. In this connection, the context of debate about community education, especially in its radical interpretation, moves outside education and into a conflation of the educational and the social in a way which has yet to be clearly defined by its advocates.

For example, the term social engineering tends to be used freely, and this raises further questions: in terms of what, and for what? Referring back to the discussion earlier about the nature of change; is there in mind some sort of para-middle-class transformation of an area? Halsey and Midwinter's stress on job and career opportunities, greater political self-determination and an enhanced quality of life go a long way towards suggesting this. Though they would disavow this, it is at the least a possible interpretation. Is the situation, then, inevitably one where politically and socially committed reformers seek to impose their pattern of change on areas where there is little inherent potential for change, in the sense of an awareness of need and a desire to act?

In summary, the notion of community education cannot be disengaged from that of compensatory education; the connections are complex and to a degree enshrouded in conflicting ideologies of educational provision in the inner city. At the same time, there is much in the community notion that is educationally positive and which suggests that, as a notion, it has more educational potential than the compensatory viewpoint. Whether this is capable of being developed as something autonomous, a genuine alternative to conventional education, will be discussed in more detail here.

Chapter 3

Community education programmes

There appear to be two broadly defined approaches which are similar in the ways they incorporate curriculum content. One of these is the community school notion which was integral with the educational priority area projects. The other has to do with using the city as a centre for learning. Both would claim to be radical alternatives to the main-stream curriculum.

The first approach has been explored in the Plowden-inspired EPA action research projects in this country, while the second is very much a North American phenomenon. Again, the first approach typifies an 'official' view of what education might be for inner-city children; it takes as its core a notion of the community school in which a community-based curriculum will be presented. The Plowden view was compensatory and conservative, but as reinterpreted by educationalists such as Midwinter, it takes on a different view of educability allied with what would count as a relevant education in the inner city. This in turn is part of a wider notion, of community regeneration, in which schools would work consciously as agents for social change in an area.

The second approach did not have its genesis in a national project but developed almost in an *ad hoc* way through the providing of educational alternatives, especially to the typical American high school. It has been very much an answer to local problems having to do with lack of money for building new schools and coping with truants and dropouts, rather than being an experiment in education in its own right.

What is to be noted about both approaches is their vulnerability as existing and being funded by local education authorities, and boards of education, alongside conventional forms of educational provision. This has meant, especially so far as the second approach is concerned, accepting the conventional goals of schooling. The intention here is to consider examples of both, with the two-fold aim of exploring their curriculum potential and implications, and also the question of whether in fact they both offer valid alternatives to the educational mainstream. Are they both genuinely radical? Can claims about their relevance be upheld?

The educational priority area projects

Briefly, the history of the EPA projects is as follows: in July 1967 the government decided to allocate £16m mainly for primary schools building renewal in the educational priority areas, which were designated according to guidelines suggested by the Plowden Committee. Parallel with this, the Urban Programme was announced by the government, in April 1968, under which between £20m and £25m would be made available for urban renewal schemes. Within this general programme, the EPA action research projects were mounted jointly by the DES and the SSRC in four areas in this country (Liverpool, Deptford, Balsall Heath and Denaby) and one in Scotland (Dundee). They were to run for three years, between 1968–71 and were granted £175,000 each for this period. Their general objective was to try to establish what were the most suitable educational development patterns for the EPAs.

Four objectives applying to all projects were decided, and these constituted their terms of reference. They were: to raise the educational performance of the children; to improve teacher morale; to increase the involvement of parents in their children's education; and to increase the sense of responsibility for their communities of the people living in them.

The major conclusions arrived at after the projects ended are listed by Halsey (1972). They are: the educational priority areas, despite difficulties in defining them, are socially and administratively viable units in which to apply the principle of positive discrimination. Pre-schooling is outstandingly the most economical and effective device to use in raising educational standards in the EPAs. The idea of the community school as outlined by the Plowden Committee has been shown to have powerful implications for community regeneration. There are practical ways of improving the partnership between families and schools in the EPAs, and practical ways of improving the quality of teaching in EPA schools. Action research has been shown to be an effective instrument for policy formation and for developing educational innovations. The EPA can be no more than a part, though an important one, of a comprehensive social movement towards community development in a modern urban industrial society.

Except indirectly, there is no mention here of curriculum content or its organisation. To some extent this reflects the autonomy of each project, in that programmes were to be mounted depending on each team's interpretation of the needs of their area. This fits the action research approach which is broadly pragmatic: strategies are tried out in order to discover what is successful and worth developing. Considering the limited budget and life span of the projects, though, they were as likely to find out what did not work without having either the time or the money to gain from this experience. This is possibly the reason why Halsey states the conclusions in such general terms, with an emphasis placed on what could, as distinct from what does, work. As a comment on this, the Liverpool project team resisted formal evaluation of its programmes, led by its director. This seems part of a wider phenomenon affecting all the projects in that little stress was placed on the evaluation of objectives themselves, although testing of children's attainment was carried out. The objectives were very general and even Halsey remarks that some of them may be question-begging, which in itself is hardly helpful in evaluation.

One apparent anomaly was the acceptance of the Plowden notion of the community school with its curriculum implications by all the projects. Yet their autonomous nature indicates that their first main task would be to diagnose the educational needs specific to their areas. It is hard to reconcile such investigations with the relatively unquestioning acceptance of the community school as a necessary part of each project; though as it happened, each project placed its own kind of emphasis on this. The other more general factor, pre-school provision, is less contentious given the long-argued need for universal pre-school education.

The projects did differ according to their areas. Broadly, Liverpool adopted and developed a community education approach which at least by implication repudiated the compensatory view. The Deptford project was essentially a combination of community education and compensatory provision in the schools. Balsall Heath's project team saw their role as compensatory. Denaby in the West Riding is more difficult to classify because of the different views held within the team itself and how these emerged as action. Its most interesting feature in the context of this study was the setting up of Red House, a social education centre. It also stressed pre-school provision and support.

What are the implications of these differences? Halsey comments that two main types of programme emerged. One dealt with clearly defined educational deficits and tended to concentrate on pre-school provision and language and mathematics enrichment. The other was concerned more with trying to change what was seen as the conservatism of schools, and of modifying teachers' attitudes, so that they could, on the project's terms, come to understand and cater for the educational needs of inner-city children. Important here are the curriculum implications and the means of arriving at agreement on how to proceed between the project and the teachers.

The Liverpool project came nearest to formulating principles on which a curriculum might be based, and some criticisms have already been made in an earlier chapter about its conclusions. At present, the major source of information about the projects is the Educational Priority series of reports.

What follows is a consideration of each project from its curriculum development viewpoint, in order to try to find out whether any curriculum principles were arrived at which could be operationalised and developed further within a community education context. The discussion may be seen in the light of Halsey's statement, that 'In all four areas curriculum development was regarded as one of the essential elements in the action research programme'.

In the Balsall Heath project, language enrichment was central partly because there were a large number of non-English-speaking children in the schools. Equipment and materials such as the SRA Reading Laboratory, Breakthrough to Literacy, and Language Masters were used in a tightly structured programme under the guidance of specially appointed remedial teachers. Thus, there were no curriculum innovations, but a more closely defined remedial–compensatory set of strategies planned in which relatively commonplace equipment was used. Significant gains were made in reading ability, especially by older junior-aged children. The community education aspect was, strictly speaking, outside the curriculum, and concentrated on liaison with parents through the work of home-school liaison teachers, whose role was to improve home-school links, to identify problems of special need, and give extra attention to especially deprived children, and to build up detailed records of families. In inducing parents to be more forthcoming to the schools about their children's problems, this operation was generally successful. The task of liaison teachers was specified by the Balsall Heath team, and it suggested that this role was as far as the concept of community education could be taken in that area at that time. While more interest was shown and more visits were made by parents to schools, there was a poor response when parents were invited to the Midlands Arts Centre where groups of children from the area were working for six week periods.

The West Riding project at Denaby also included language enrichment programmes but these were distinctively remedial and designed for older junior-aged children who were non-readers. The population was stable and included very few non-English-speaking children. The approach resembled that devised by the Balsall Heath team. Again, it was very much the case of relatively familiar equipment being used by trained remedial teachers in a closely structured programme and with a greater concentration on assessment of results than is usual in primary schools. The results were variable, the best ones coming from tests which were most closely related to the style of the programme and its content. Again, the community education aspect was not strictly speaking in the curriculum. It focused on Red House, a community centre with residential places. It provided opportunities for teachers and students to work intensively with small groups of children, though the results of this aspect of the project were not assessed or intended to be. The concept of Red House was that of a community centre serving schools, putting on courses as desired by parents, and as a sanctuary for children when there were serious but temporary family difficulties. There is some indication that it did provide a forum and meeting place for parents, children, and teachers, but its effects on schooling and on curriculum development are virtually impossible to identify.

The Deptford scheme was more complex, and more innovatory. It was the project which singularly typified the uneasy balance between compensatory approaches and community education which is implicit in the Plowden recommendations. The team tried to develop a curriculum which began with a basic community education premise, that of involving parents in their children's schooling, as well as developing language and mathematics enrichment programmes. In the published conclusions it is difficult to tell which aspect or aspects were seen as most important by the team. Unlike the Liverpool project which in part it resembled, detailed testing of children's attainment and attitudes to school was undertaken by an evaluator who was not a project member. One feature which distinguishes this project from the others was the attention paid to the teachers' role and function within it, in trying to achieve the laid-down objectives. The director, quoted by Halsey, said: 'It was considered essential that head teachers were seen as part of our team. The emphasis would be on strengthening and re-evaluating their role within the school environment and influencing them to become agents of social change in the neighbourhood community . . . So, the emphasis would be on support for the teachers with the underlying principle of self-propagation.'

This highlights a current debate about curriculum change which has been discussed by Skilbeck (1971) and Hoyle (1969; 1971) and usefully summed up by MacDonald and Walker (1976). Skilbeck contends that genuine change can only happen at the grassroots level, through the activities of teachers and not through curriculum engineering in the form of projects introduced by agencies outside the schools. This is reflected in curriculum development in the shift from centrally organised curriculum projects to a concern with small-scale school and classroom-based development. The Deptford attempt to get through to the teachers demonstrates an accurate assessment of the situation: the Deptford teachers had a lower morale compared with teachers in the other three projects; it also indicates a particular view of the nature of curriculum change and the position of the change agent.

The question is, to what extent did this attempted collaboration produce a predominantly compensatory-type programme, or one which was more in line with the community education concept. The project included elements of both, and according to the test results obtained on children's achievement and attitude towards school, neither approach could claim success. The indication is that the two emphases were not reconciled and that the project suffered because of unresolved differences.

A large-scale environmental studies project involving four hundred older junior children and many of their parents using a field studies centre at Swanley in Kent was a focal point for the whole programme. Discovery-based learning was encouraged; it used aids such as a teachers' manual, maps, descriptions of walks, and suggestions as to how various topics might be studied. There were two related aims: that language, mathematics, science, and art and craft as representing normal primary school subjects would be used as the means for studying the area so that children would develop a new interest in them through this different context; and that children's perceptions of environment would develop through this programme to a point where they would be enabled to compare Deptford with the rural environment of Kent, which in turn would foster a sense of social awareness for their own area. Tests subsequently administered showed that children's attitudes to school had not changed significantly compared with those of a control group, nor were there any significant differences in English or mathematics attainment. However, these did not accord with teachers' views. They felt that the children had developed a more positive attitude towards school as a result of their experiences. But the expected development in children's perceptions did not emerge. It has been suggested that because of unresolved problems in the design of the project that little by way of tangible results could be expected of it (Barnes, 1975).

The mathematics programme concentrated on developing in teachers further understanding of primary mathematics and teaching approaches. The language programme was developed jointly by the project team, teachers, and local inspectors, and again the emphasis was on making teachers more competent in promoting language development. The testing included interviewing teachers, who in general felt that the programme as a whole had been successful.

The Deptford project remains the most tantalising of the four, with its prime goal, to involve teachers in curriculum development and to modify their attitudes to change, and in the attempt to integrate compensatory-type schemes with those having a community education rationale. This represents an attempt to reconcile the short-term objectives usually attributed to compensatory strategies with the long-term ones attaching to community education. Other provisions included students from a local college of education working with children in small groups and on a one-to-one basis to facilitate attainment and a more positive attitude towards learning. Liaison agents were appointed and two school premises were made available to parents and children during evenings for a variety of activities. The project demonstrably ran out of time partly because of internal tensions which can be attributed to the failure to resolve the compensatory with the community aspects. There were disagreements, mainly unvoiced, it would appear between what the team and the teachers saw as being the project – its rationale, its objectives, and what it was attempting to achieve. For these reasons it is important to this discussion and it will be examined in more detail in the form of a case study in a later chapter.

The Liverpool project was community education-based. It has received more publicity than the others because of its imaginative work and its charismatic director. Arguably, it went further than other projects in developing a community-based curriculum, and thereby shifting the Plowden compensatory emphasis to a community education context. Direct concern with improving children's grasp of basic skills was subordinated to a number of curriculum innovations. Among these were the creation of a supermarket in one school which became the focal point for projects involving mathematics and creative activities; a local environment survey which enlisted college students to work with children in exploring and reporting on their neighbourhood; a study of local institutions; infant school mathematics schemes; and creative work based on festivals throughout the year. As already mentioned there was considerable parental involvement and publicity of schools' work through displays, in local shops and the distribution of school news sheets.

The general conclusions which the team drew from their work have been discussed. But there was no testing by an external evaluator on the scale of the Deptford project. Indeed, an anti-testing bias can be detected. Midwinter (1972c) comments: 'One hopes that the findings will be of value, but they are not the consequences of a pure and controlled laboratory investigation. They have been very carefully garnered and assessed, but the trap of offering half-baked superficial figures has, one hopes, been avoided.'

Even taking Halsey's point, that the effects of a community-based curriculum can only be seen in the long-term, and that conventional means of assessment are inappropriate, an opportunity to investigate children's attitudes, and to discover for instance whether their perceptions of their neighbourhood had changed as a result of the project's work seems to have been lost. The project therefore, as a project about the possibility of a community curriculum resides in something of a research vacuum.

Despite the claims made in the Midwinter interpretation, it is not clear to what extent the programme was truly community-orientated.

On the face of it, the community notion was dominant but there are only descriptive accounts of what went on to substantiate this claim. Again, Halsey's comments are significant: he asserts that the precondition for community education is the community-based curriculum, which at present, to quote him, is at 'a rather primitive stage'.

The American experience

It has been suggested, by Jenkins and Raggatt (1974) for example, that the problems which large American cities now face may well be a feature of cities in this country in a decade's time. The contexts are different, as are the issues which are likely to reproduce the problems: in the USA the wider gap between rich and poor; differential qualities of education due to local control and provision; a social democratic philosophy which allows considerably less intervention than is the case here when deprivation and need are identified. In summary, the conditions are less extreme – less polarised – here. But the similarities are strong enough to provoke an examination of the community focus of alternative schools in the USA as providing some possible indicators for the direction of urban development here. This becomes more compelling when a piecemeal, 'social studies' interpretation of community education seems increasingly to be accepted by educators here as the legitimate form, setting aside a more radical view.

Jenkins and Raggatt in discussing research studies mounted by the Center for New Schools in Chicago, mention three features which are characteristic of alternative high schools. These are, first, they tend to be urban schools; second, they have an intake policy which ensures ethnically mixed school populations; and third, they are concerned primarily with the problems found in poor areas. As to their community focus, these originate in the thinking of de-schoolers such as Illich, in emphasising the potential of the city as a learning resource. But a crucial difference compared with the de-schoolers lies in the fact that they are conceived of as schools, with a defined population and teachers on the payroll, but also drawing upon other professionals found in the city, and their areas of professional concern such as museums, factories, offices, laboratories, parks, and zoos. Illich's educational networks therefore are the major part of the school, but not the school in totality. Gumbert (1971) makes this point in his discussion of alternative schools. He also in his argument reverses the Midwinter contention that schools must be agencies for social change. He is much more concerned with the pedagogy: pupils would draw upon community resources rather than the community focusing upon the school.

Perhaps the most well-known of the American alternative high schools is the Parkway Program in Philadelphia. The reasons for founding it in 1969 owed more to financial stringency than educational experimentation. By 1967 it was clear that a new high school would be needed in Philadelphia because of population growth and overcrowding. The Board of Education did not have the money to provide a building and there were also pressing problems of dropout among students.

The campus is the Benjamin Franklin Parkway in which is situated most of the city's cultural institutions. The Board accepted the proposal for the setting up of a 'school without walls' and appointed John Bremer, who had been the educational director of a community controlled school in New York, as its Director of Program. In their discussion, Farrington, Pritchard and Raynor (1973) outline the strategies and organisation. Community resources were to be used as fully as possible and the core here was the use of community teachers to teach specialised courses. Parents were included as consultants. Students would be responsible directly for their own education; they would plan their own timetables. Students also would take a part in course evaluation by commenting on their own attainment and that of the teachers.

There were four separate units each with its own headquarters in different parts of the city but these were not conceived of as teaching spaces; they provided office space for administration and a communal room and lockers for students. In 1971–72 there were approximately 200 students in each unit and a staff of ten full time qualified teachers whose job it was to cover the range of subjects required in order for students to gain a Pennsylvania State Diploma. Because of a very wide and diverse number of programmes, some means by which students could be enabled to relate the components was necessary, and thus a tutorial system was used as being the only compulsory element in a student's programme. The tutorial group comprises about fifteen students with a teacher and a student teacher. The tutorials provide help for students in course planning, evaluation, choosing appropriate goals, and solving problems as they occur. It is interesting to note that the tutorial group is also a basic skills imparting unit, so that students receive tuition in language and mathematics as well as undertaking their chosen courses of study.

Community teachers are drawn from those who are in a position to provide courses asked for; they are not paid; on the whole it appears that they are both efficient teachers as well as being enthusiastic in imparting their knowledge. Each community teacher is linked to a certificated teacher who advises on methods, attendance, evaluation, and discipline. Farrington, Pritchard and Raynor consider that these teachers do present problems to do with teaching expertise. This is perhaps inevitable, not necessarily because they are working as untrained teachers but because they have the task of reconciling their teaching function with their normal job demands.

There are problems within the programme itself: truancy, the pressures on teachers to learn a new conception of teaching, student choice and its management, and the sheer logistical problems of integrating the whole enterprise. There is also the pressure which students experience in making the transfer from one style of schooling to another, and trying to come to terms with the freedom and responsibility which the Parkway Program entails. A proportion of students find these demands too great and they either drop out or re-enter a conventional high school.

A similar school is the Chicago Public High School for Metropolitan Studies, known as Metro High School. It was roughly contemporary with the Parkway Program, and took it as its model. The intake is composed of volunteers from other Chicago high schools and the object was to represent as closely as possible the ethnic, socioeconomic and geographical mix which exists in Chicago. Like the Parkway Program, it utilises city resources in the form of community teachers, institutions, businesses and other community and professional associations for its curriculum content and teaching.

Its origins rested more firmly on educational thinking than was the case with the Parkway Program. It grew out of suggestions put forward by the Urban Research Corporation which was concerned with alternatives to the conventional 'tracked' system of American high schools. The main alternative is a 'pathway' curriculum, determined by the student working with guidance and being responsible for following his chosen programme.

The sorts of problems which Metro High School met are not surprisingly, similar to those encountered by the Parkway Program. One has to do with the curriculum. There is a very wide range of courses, noted in the 'Catalog of Offerings', which include staff-run courses and those located in some 150 businesses, and cultural and community bodies. At the same time, the Chicago Board of Education suggested a broad curriculum division, of skills, humanities and social sciences, and natural sciences which amounted to a faculty concept. It is hard to see how this, and what is included in the programme can be reconciled in practice. Indeed, this original specification underlined the fact that Metro was seen by the Board as an experiment; it had to function within the structure of the Chicago Board of Education and be appraised alongside conventional schools. Jenkins and Raggatt mention what was a serious political challenge to its existence which was unresolved at their time of writing (1974) with the appointment of a district superintendent who in effect refused to recognise the school's experimental status.

Other earlier problems had had to do with staff–student decision making. Various methods were tried out to set up effective machinery which would be acceptable to all. The first was a weekly all-school meeting known as the Administrative Board. It proved to be unwieldy for its function and was replaced by a more flexibly interpreted device where any five students who felt that they were a legitimate 'interest group' could send a member to represent them at the Administrative Board. However, this was no more successful, and eventually the more conventional vehicle of the staff meeting and related committees took over the decision-making responsibilities.

Jenkins and Raggatt also consider a general difficulty of the 'school without walls' – the isolation of students and the problem of contact and communication:

'The school-without-walls disperses students, often in natural groupings, through the city. Communications are difficult, and students rarely meet to speak with one collective voice. When we were there, the noticeboard was obliterated with several hundred nondescript notices. At times, this commitment to dispersal results in the loneliness of the long-distance learner, propelled out into the dazzling city like a ball in a pinball machine, striking objects and picking up credits, forever riding the subway and the elevated railway.' (p. 51.)

In considering these problems Newmann and Oliver's (1967) exploration of learning contexts is an attempt to develop a conceptual structure for alternative forms of education. Though they were writing before the Parkway Program and Metro High School and many others had been founded, what they have to say is relevant to the problems and the possibilities. They suggest that there are three distinct contexts in which learning goes on: first, the *school context* which has to do with basic skills and which will be concerned with systematic teaching and learning. Given that it will be systematic, they suggest a greater range of methods and uses of equipment than is usually found in schools, yet they claim that this context with its relatively narrow range is the only one recognised in conventional school systems.

The second context they term *laboratory-studio-work*. The emphasis here is on problem-centred learning by which they understand '. . . the solution of problems which the learner wants to attack, regardless of educational by-products that dealing with the problem might bring'. The physical siting might be in a school, a museum, a factory or a laboratory: that is, wherever the problem can be identified, understood and solved by the student. The range of possibilities they suggest as

examples resembles the courses offered both by the Parkway Program
and Metro High School.

The third context they call the *community seminar context*. Here, the
purpose is to gather concerned individuals together in order to study
community issues. It would include students, professionals of various
kinds, and indeed anyone who can focus meaning upon the sorts of
issues which Newmann and Oliver would expect to be discussed in
seminars. Again, it is not simply a matter of reflecting and discussing:
'The major thrust of the seminars would be reflection and deliberation,
though the questions discussed would be highly relevant to the laboratory
context or the world of "action".'

In summary then, they see education as having three facets: systematic
instruction, action, and reflection. They occur concurrently and are not
confined to school students.

If these are to become part of school learning then radical shifts in
attitudes and roles will be required of teachers and administrators. They
suggest that teachers are the best qualified to operate as instructors but
that others will be concerned in the laboratory and seminar contexts.
They envisage the sort of tapping of human and cultural resources that
alternative high schools have attempted. Moreover, they make the
important point that this is not community education in the community-
specific sense; it is an education 'in community' in response to a growing
commonality of issues and problems as communication and transport-
ation methods grow more sophisticated.

This attempt at formulating a conceptual framework goes much of
the way towards providing practical solutions to pedagogical problems.
The major difficulty, however, is political and bureaucratic. It has to do
with the decision-making policies of governing and funding bodies
which also are providing conventional schools. Alternative forms of
education will appear where the mainstream has failed, and if they
succeed they lose their *raison d'etre*. This sounds paradoxical – the
point has to do with the degree of difference allowable in the curricula
of the alternative high schools and their funding by boards of education.
Given the wide curriculum of the American high school, that of its
alternatives differ more in style and in the learning contexts. Both the
Parkway Program and Metro High School retain the traditional
accolade of the American high school – graduation, and with it the
possiblity of students furthering their education. This needs to be seen
not only as a requirement of the boards of education concerned, but
recognition on the part of the schools of the educational expectations of
students. If the alternative schools are by and large successful, both with
students who reject conventional education and with those who simply

find the freedom of choice more conducive to their success, then the schools are likely to cease to be experimental and will in time become legitimised. This has not yet begun, but as modified forms of the first generation develop, there is a strong likelihood that they will be accepted as being valid parallel institutions alongside conventional schools. Already some changes, especially in their internal government, suggest that a form of alternative is emerging where the pedagogical style differs only. Academic goals are the same for both types; the use of community resources has in the first place, a financial appeal for hard-pressed Boards of Education, and in the second, a potential for socialising students to accept the values of their society, through learning which is both the student's choice, and is in the hands of significant members of the student's society. Indeed, the alternative school is likely to be more influential than conventional schools in the second of these, since it exposes students to their own society through a form of open education unique in developed school systems, rather than isolating them as do conventional schools.

It is not inconceivable that high schools will adopt those aspects of the alternative schools which do not involve major reappraisals of their organisation of learning and teaching, and the consequent professional anxiety caused to staff and administrators, if only to provide an educational experience acceptable to those students who would normally drop out. In this country, one can cite the RoSLA programme courses in many comprehensives as being a very modest step in the same direction.

It cannot be denied that the few experimental alternative schools are radical; that is, they are as radical as their local administrators, and their students, will allow them to be. As Farrington, Pritchard and Raynor say about the Parkway Program: 'It is of course, most unlikely that schools along the lines of Parkway will be widely adopted, so its value in educational change would seem to lie in the fact that it can serve as a model whose experimentation has implications for urban schooling in general.'

As to the questions first posed here, the context of both the EPA projects and those of the alternative high schools is much the same. They emerged as possible answers to educational crisis, and the manner of their funding has meant that they have been obliged to adopt the conventional goals of schooling within a framework of learning and teaching which is different from that in conventional schools. This says much about external pressures on goals, whatever the form of schooling; it also comments on what is seen to count as criteria for educability. The American experiment, at face value, provides more answers if questions about curricula relevance are asked. Farrington, Pritchard and Raynor raise the question: what is a genuine community curriculum? 'A distinction has to be made between a community-located curriculum where learning can take place in any part of the city, and a community-based curriculum where much of the learning is about the city. A community-located curriculum which is not community-based fails to utilise the urban potential to its fullest extent.' They claim that Parkway has a genuine community curriculum because it draws upon the community for its learning experiences, and it is attuned to living in the urban setting. This constitutes a relevant community urban education. Can the same be said of the action research projects? Where the alternative high schools have tried to adopt, in Popper's terms, a radical solution, the EPA projects have chosen a piecemeal notion of reform, with the possible exception of the Liverpool project, which will be examined in more detail in the next chapter.

Both approaches are recent, and are still developing. Of the two, the concept of the alternative high school is the more radical. The EPA projects have been criticised here because they do not seem to have produced much by way of directions or criteria for a relevant, alternative urban education. Their association with the compensatory viewpoint has also to be borne in mind. The question that is as yet unanswered is, whether either approach has forged for itself a sufficiently distinct identity which will allow further development alongside the educational mainstream, or whether they will eventually converge with it.

Chapter 4

The present concept of the community-based curriculum

The notion of community

It has been claimed that the focal point of community education is the community-based curriculum. But before considering the nature, or for that matter the possibility of an education which is linked to the community, the notion of 'community' itself needs to be examined. It is an elusive notion which has yielded broad definitions having questionable application. One might consider the Seebohm Committee's definition as an example: 'The notion of a community implies the existence of a network of reciprocal social relationships, which among other things ensure mutual aid and give those who experience it a sense of well-being.' This refers to the first of two broad interpretations: the sense of belonging to a group; and having to do with the network of social relationships existing within a defined geographical area.

There are various problems connected with attempts at definitions. Among these are, whether in fact a sense of community exists in any strongly identifiable way in the inner city; whether local community problems can be identified and possible solutions devised; or whether these are in fact overshadowed by more general characteristics such as unemployment, low standard housing, low incomes and poor educational provision.

Questions such as these highlight the possible ambiguities of the term. Hill (1972) has drawn attention to the two broad interpretations outlined here, which tend to coalesce in simple agrarian societies, and to the debate among sociologists about the extent to which modern urban societies differ from agrarian societies in this respect. The outcome of such a debate should throw light on whether or not a form of education which is described as community education is possible, or indeed valid, in urban areas. The argument is by no means resolved, however. Some sociologists claim that urban society is characterised by impersonality and anonymity; others claim that identifiable communities do exist in cities in much the same way as they exist in rural areas. Hill, citing Pahl (1970), advances the idea that the notion of community as applied to urban and especially inner city areas can be misleading and simplistic and the descriptive term 'locality social system' might be preferable.

Such a description tends to move towards the second general interpretation, which has to do with social interrelations in a geographical
area. It under-emphasises the affective side, which the Seebohm
Committee's definition stresses. If the notion is reduced to that of social
interplay in an area, this moves away from the view that people living
in it will have a sense of identity with it; there will be shared values,
beliefs and procedures only to the extent that they are needed for the day-
to-day transactions between people living in close proximity. This view,
of an instrumental framework for everyday activities poses serious questions as to whether community education can be a meaningful concept.

Hill suggests three differences in the urban setting where it is compared
with the rural. Firstly, that an individual's claim to membership of a
community usually refers to a small part – perhaps only two or three
streets – of a more extensive area. Secondly, there is no clear commonality between where individuals live and the social networks to which
they belong. Thirdly, the community as such will probably not correspond with politically or administratively defined areas, nor is there any
consistency in the way that these correspond with areas of employment
or retail marketing. Again, some material from research should illustrate
the implications which follow from Hill's points, which are the very real
problems of achieving credibility for the notion of community in the
Seebohm sense at least when it is applied to inner-city areas. Coates and
Silburn's study of the St Anne's district of Nottingham is relevant here.
The neighbourhood was split over issues to do with redevelopment. The
shop-keepers and owner occupiers wished to see improvement and
renewal and refurbishing of the area as it existed. Tenants on the other
hand, wished to see wholesale redevelopment to provide new housing.

In considering the question as to whether general characteristics tend
to override what might be distinctive of an area, Benington's work (1973)
is illustrative. His study concerned the possible redevelopment of the
Hillfields area of Coventry, which was one of the twelve areas designated
within the Home Office Community Development Project. He arrives at
three tentative conclusions, or propositions, having to do with the interpretation of needs at the official level in a deprived inner-city area, which
are likely to have far-reaching implications for the question of what is to
count as community education in such areas. Firstly, local and central
government agencies seem to work on the assumption that there is a
homogeneity of need in areas. Secondly, central government lays down
norms according to which categories of people are defined in assessing
their level of deprivation. Inner-city problems to do with social deprivation are seen as the results of bureaucratic mistakes in planning, and
solutions will be found by plugging gaps in the social services. More
fundamentally, deprivation is seen in terms of assumed disabilities which

have the effect of preventing people from benefitting from the services available. This is the classic 'cycle of deprivation' interpretation. Furthermore, there is an unintentional reinforcement of this intrinsic deprivation notion built into the way in which the Supplementary Benefits Commission works. The 'poor' are designated as such according to criteria laid down which may have little to do with actual, experienced poverty. As Benington comments:

'*We have a hunch this operates in many other situations as well, and consequently we need to be alert to what in fact we as community workers are doing to groups of people and neighbourhoods in accepting and acting on labels like "social priority areas" or "deprived groups". The mere bringing of such neighbourhoods or such groups into the orbit of official definitions, and also official stances, reinforces their stigmatisation and perpetuates the problems.*' (p. 177.)

Thirdly, he contends that an increasing range of issues are being taken out of public debate and treated as if they were matters for social science. This represents a generalist approach to problems of deprivation rather than the area-specific approach which he is defending. As a consequence, broad characteristics are attributed to an area and these are used as a basis for presumed amelioration.

Clearly, these points have important implications for how community education may be interpreted and what will be seen as being a good 'fit' between community education programmes and policies and the neighbourhood in which they are sited. What needs to be recalled in this context is the position of the action research projects. Areas were designated as educational priority areas; action research projects were directed to these, by the central government acting upon the recommendations and the criteria proposed by a national enquiry body: the Plowden Committee. Furthermore, the projects themselves were encapsulated in the Urban Aid programme.

The situation, given Benington's conclusions is that the normal procedure will be for programmes to be devised by teams of professionals which perforce will adopt this generalist social engineering standpoint. There will be some limited room for manoeuvre within the areas themselves but to talk about project teams' 'autonomy' in such a context is meaningless. So far as the educational experience itself is concerned, on the one hand there is the assumption that conditions will be much the same as between areas; but on the other hand, much emphasis was placed, in two of the projects, on children's developing awareness of what was special about their own environment. There are, surely, tensions here between practice and policy, both at the project team planning, and the central planning levels.

It must be asked, then, can an educational programme which takes as its official basis assumed common characteristics in inner-city areas which must be changed, also take account of possible differences in different areas? The EPA project teams seemed able to do this, in a limited way which has been discussed earlier. It is surely the case though, that there will be a considerable range of differences in different areas. Questions are raised as to whether project workers will be enabled, firstly to perceive these differences, and secondly, arrive at independent decisions as to whether or not they require their attention. Some may present pressing demands for change; others may not.

The notion of community, then, presents general problems of interpretation and special ones concerning the nature of community education. Keller's (1966) discussion extends these difficulties by shifting the debate to a consideration of 'neighbourhood' which resembles Pahl's 'locality social system'. She discusses three dimensions: cognitive, utilitarian, and affective, in terms of which people living in a neighbourhood might perceive it. These amount to how people identify with an area; how a defined group uses facilities in an area; and how people feel about an area. Two main questions provide the guidelines for her enquiry: according to existing evidence, how much and what kinds of neighbouring occur in different types of settlements, and what factors account for the patterns found? Also, what evidence is there for the existence of neighbourhoods in modern urban settings? Her general conclusion is that the concept is harder to distinguish at work in urban areas compared with small towns and villages. The urban area is characterised by fragmentation, except in the case of the poorest and most immobile inhabitants, who of necessity rely more on support provided by fellow inhabitants. This, however, is a relative phenomenon. Their neighbourhood 'sense' is still weaker and less easy to distinguish compared with that felt by people living in villages and small towns.

What underlines her conclusions is the negative nature of this sense of neighbouring, depending as it does on everyday necessity. It is essentially fatalistic and its perspectives do not depart from the day-to-day problems of living in the inner city. They do not permit any reliable notion developing of the possibility of change.

Ashcroft's (1973) discussion of the major models of community development and their educational implications reinforces the view here, that the basis for any cogent statement about the nature of community education and its workings is decidedly shaky, given the elusiveness of the notion of 'community' coupled with what seems to be agreement that it is difficult, at the least, to apply it meaningfully to the inner city. He suggests that there are three main models of community development. Advocates of the *universal* model would argue that there is a lack of community-mindedness among all sections of society. The model has both radical and conservative origins, and from these derive two dimensions: firstly, 'universal' theorists usually evoke an earlier, golden age, where individuals understood their role in society and where anomy was unknown. Secondly, the need for political and cultural regeneration is claimed as being necessary for combating anomy. Decision-making processes will happen at the local level and will involve as many people as possible.

The second model, the *mainstream* is concerned exclusively with the problems of the poor. It is this model which has informed attempts to develop community education programmes in this country and the USA. The problems of inner-city people are seen as being two-fold: lack of job opportunities and good-quality housing, and inadequate educational and recreational facilities. Accompanying this is the attitude which such conditions engender, and which forms a closed circle: poverty produces its own culture, which is inter-generational. It is Shumsky's (1968) 'psychological meaning of poverty'. Mainstream community development recognises local conditions. Solutions to problems will be found in the immediate neighbourhood. But Ashcroft comments:

'*More often however there is a somewhat illogical conjunction of societal diagnosis with neighbourhood solution. First let us consider societal diagnosis. It is perfectly clear that many of the poor areas usually suffer from widespread unemployment. It is equally clear that the creation of more employment opportunities has depended ultimately upon* major *capital investment decisions made either by large firms or by central government, the latter usually taking the form of subsidies to private or public enterprise in return for investment in poor regions. Moreover in Western Europe the creation of "the regional fund" within the EEC means that such decisions may well be made internationally; so that in practice, north-eastern England will be competing with southern Italy for scarce capital to resolve its problems.*' (p. 26.)

He claims that:

'*Local solutions to problems of such magnitude are irrelevant. Even acting as vigorous pressure groups, at national or international level, Community Development Projects cannot be of much significance. . . . It is precisely this impotence, even if honestly recognised, that makes community developers fall back on neighbourhood solutions.*' (p. 26.)

Thirdly, he considers the *radical* model. Advocates of this would claim that the universal model is useful in helping to diagnose the illness in a general way but that its causes will be beyond that viewpoint's powers of amelioration. The mainstream model is criticised for its compensatory perspective, symbolised by the use of terms such as 'deprived' and 'underprivileged' to describe the poor. The view is taken that the poor are exploited by the wealthy in order for the wealthy to preserve the *status quo*. The solution lies in strong grassroots political movements in which the oppressed are concerned with challenging the mechanisms by which they are oppressed and those who operate them, rather than the application of 'Band-aid'-type measures which characterise the first two models.

The interpretation of education differs as the three models differ in their perception of need. Universal model community education is concerned with relating the school to the local community. This appears in fact to be developing as the officially accepted view of community education. The mainstream model focuses upon the poor in a society. The view here is that community education emerges primarily as a response to the failure of compensatory programmes. This view of community education resembles that mounted in the Liverpool EPA project especially, and in the Deptford project in a more limited way. Ashcroft sees it in terms of access to school facilities, and resources for community use, and is sceptical about the possibility, within this interpretation, of a community-based curriculum being developed. The radical form has to do with alternatives to the educational mainstream; by implication, it repudiates institutionalised 'safe' interpretations of community education.

Community and education

The substance of the discussion so far is that a definition of 'community' is at the least elusive and at the most, impossible to state except in a general way. The Seebohm Committee's definition may represent all that is feasible. In fact it might be argued that the search for a more precise specification is unrealistic, given the serious doubts that exist as to whether, or to what extent, a sense of community exists in the inner city.

But if this is all that is possible, what of community education? At this point, some clarification as to its perceived nature is called for with the aim of identifying a dominant or an emerging interpretation. Hatch and Moylan (1972) see the community school as extending the school's role so that the school-community distinction becomes blurred. They suggest that this can be accomplished in either a radical or a moderate way. The first would entail the school becoming an agent for social change through community development. A two-way process would be ensured by the presence of the community in the school, in its curriculum, and in local communal control.

The second, moderate way which they trace to the Plowden Committee's thinking, sees the school's facilities being made available outside school hours and perhaps during them. There would be a sharing of community services and the school premises (but perhaps not the school) would be the community's focal point.

It would seem that the dominant idea at present of community education, though not necessarily the community school, is closer to Hatch and Moylan's moderate interpretation. Forms of community activity which involve older secondary pupils have been accepted by schools. They include, for example, visiting old people in the area, hospital visiting, helping to care for pre-school-aged children, and other part-time social work of this kind. There is no necessary two-way relationship in this, which characterises the radical interpretation. Change, if it is there at all, seems to figure implicitly but tends not to be thought of either as a basis for reconsidering the given curriculum, or as a coherent replacement for it. Rather, this kind of community involvement is seen both as ancillary to, and a modification of, the given curriculum, depending upon how willingly or otherwise pupils accept the customary bill of fare. The proposals made by Colin and Meg Ball (1973) are a good illustration of the involvement interpretation which accords with the moderate view.

Furthermore, this occupies only one part of education. It is very much a secondary school phenomenon. The Balls are strongly concerned with the reaction of potential early leavers who reject the traditional school curriculum as being irrelevant, and they see involvement of this kind as being more meaningful educationally for the RoSLA group. Hatch and Moylan's survey of secondary schools which claimed to be community schools showed that many included this sort of involvement, which was taken as a main defining characteristic. The Balls make a plea for much more.

This is a notion of community education which is becoming established in secondary schools; what form community schools might take in the future is a more open question. What is important is that a community activity conception is developing as the legitimate interpretation both of community education, and as the most significant characteristic of the community school. Arguably, it has its merits. Equally arguably, it is at most a superficial notion, concentrating as it does on various social education alternatives for young school leavers and voluntary social work involvement for older secondary pupils. Certainly, this is so when it is contrasted with Hatch and Moylan's radical interpretation, which parallels the Halsey-Midwinter view. It will be useful at this point to consider in more detail the radical view which claims to offer a coherent alternative education with long-term social goals, in contrast with what is developing as the accepted view of community education. The discussion needs to be seen against the backdrop of the problematic notion of community, and also the point which has been considered in some detail here, and which Ashcroft also has made: the emergence of community education schemes as alternatives to the failure of compensatory programmes in the inner city.

The community school and the community-based curriculum

Midwinter, along with Halsey claims that a major goal is that of making children familiar with as many aspects of their immediate environment as possible. The socially-orientated curriculum is defined by Midwinter (1972b) as 'the exercise of social skills on related social materials'. He stresses the claim of greater relevance for the social as against the academic curriculum. Community regeneration is acknowledged as the long-term aim but there are shorter-term objectives. In the following passage quoted, Midwinter (1972b) sets out his attempt to do three things: to justify that a community-based curriculum is valuable in itself; to argue its value as preparation for later involvement and identification with the community; and to make the claim that such a curriculum will also facilitate the learning of basic skills:

'The community-oriented curriculum has three possible subsidiary advantages beyond the prior, long term hope for a higher level of civic participation. First, it is likely that given a socially-oriented content, children will do as well, and probably better in traditional attainments, simply because the exercise of their reading, writing and so on will be directly geared to their experience. This answers a much-pressed criticism of social education i.e. the suggestion that "academic" prowess suffers. Second, the child is dignified by the acceptance that education can be about him and his environs, that he is an historical character in a geographical situation with social, spiritual, technical and other problems facing him. The ceaseless wandering off to the cowsheds of rurality or the poesy of yesteryear can be a constant reminder to the child that "education" is by implication not of his world. Third, parental involvement and support for curricular enterprises would probably be enhanced by a socially relevant curriculum, in that the parents' own experience, occupations, insights and so forth would be material evidence. The mysteries of the school would be, in part, replaced by a substance well-known to the parent.' (p. 29.)

This presupposes much. Firstly, that junior-aged children will have the maturity to be aware of the social implications of the curriculum.

Midwinter (1972b) claims that even seven- and eight-year-olds demonstrate that they have this maturity through their acceptance for example, of family responsibilities and in the competence they display in managing these. But, there is a difference between being able to cope with the care of younger brothers and sisters, shopping, and other errands, by being brought up to expect to do these things following the example set by older children in the family and parents' expectations; and becoming aware of the community in the sense of being equipped to examine it from what will be an analytical and prescriptive viewpoint. There is a confusion here between a bogus maturity force-fed by circumstances, and maturity which takes place according to broad-based developmental processes at work. The examples which Midwinter (1972b) gives tend to underline this confusion.

Secondly, even if all is as Midwinter describes it, the content material is likely to do no more than provide the medium through which conventional primary school skills learning will take place. It is of course unexceptional to claim that children will learn more readily if they are exposed to content drawn from their everyday experience. This is a basic tenet of child-centred education. It might also be the case that children will develop an awareness of their environment which will take on a critical connotation, but no evidence is advanced by Midwinter as to how or whether children, through being exposed to a socially-orientated curriculum, do develop awareness of this kind. The notion seems essentially to be an adult one, which invests peculiar properties in curriculum content which must become part of the children's *mise en scène* through their being exposed to it. There is much of the abstractionist account of learning in this, which Dearden (1967) has criticised in his discussion of discovery methods in primary education.

Furthermore, an assumption seems to be made that the 'academic' curriculum inevitably takes as its content material which is outside the children's experiences, and which has seen little change since the days of elementary schooling. This is implausible, considering the wide range of curriculum and organisational innovations in primary schools. These include new teaching and learning approaches in mathematics, science, topic and project work, environmental studies, art and craft, and in the teaching of reading. Along with these there have been widespread organisational changes such as unstreaming, vertical grouping, integrated day working, and team and cooperative teaching.

Another assumption is made, about parents' receptivity of a social curriculum. Midwinter (1972a) has commented adversely on the traditional view of schooling which he maintains most parents hold. By implication they are likely to distrust unfamiliar forms of education. However, the changes mentioned above have been taking place over a long period of time in infant and junior schools and are generally accepted characteristics of primary education in this country.

It can be claimed that schools will be accepted by parents if they are seen as authoritative and professional institutions, however they are organised, which their children attend according to given terms of reference, and where attainments can be demonstrated.

But what is distinctive about the community-based curriculum? How does it differ from the mainstream? Midwinter (1972c) has said much about its ethos, and a little about its framework. He has also restated the terms of reference of the traditional subjects in the primary school from a social and community viewpoint. History is: 'the illumination of the present, the here and now, by the past, that it might be lived in more fruitfully'. Geography is: 'the placing of the present, the here and now, in its context, that it might be lived in more fruitfully'. Religious education is: 'the discussion of the moral and spiritual problems, posed by the present, the here and now, that it might be lived in more fruitfully'. Science is: 'the understanding of the technical structure of the present, the here and now, that it might be lived in more fruitfully'.

Since this smacks more of incantation than definition, it does not take us much further. He goes on to consider the conceptual limitations which the majority of junior-school-aged children display in these subject areas, and which need to be taken account of however they are taught. To summarise: historically, an inability to distinguish between past and present with any consistency. Geographically, an inability to understand space beyond walking and short travelling distances; difficulties in understanding scientific principles, and the abstract ideas implicit in religious education content. Research into the nature of conceptual understanding, as carried out by Piaget and his colleagues, for example, bear out these observations.

But so far as the community-based curriculum and its aims are concerned, there are two connected problems. The first concerns the nature of this restatement of the curriculum and its potential for achieving its aims, while the second casts doubts as to whether anything that is distinctive of a community-based curriculum has been said.

In the first place, although Midwinter (1972b) is willing to accept these conclusions into conceptual development and understanding, and in fact sees them as a reinforcement for the sort of curriculum he is advocating, he, at the same time, wants to claim that the young junior-school-aged child is, in his words, 'ready to examine his community thoroughly . . . some people underrate the social capacity of junior children in educational priority areas. One never ceases to be amazed at their resilience and social aplomb, at the mature manner with which they cope with social situations and problems that might test the emotional and intellectual stamina of many an adult'. Earlier, the confusion between a genuine social maturity and an apparent social awareness, based on family expectations of the role of older children within it was commented upon. This now can be looked at against a broader educational background, given what Midwinter (1972b) has to say about the social reinterpretation of the mainstream curriculum and its developmental constraints. He seems to be claiming a level of developmental understanding in a social-environmental context which cannot be claimed for historical, geographical, scientific or religious education contexts; that somehow, proximity to the subject matter induces more intellectual maturity than study of content at a further remove. This raises questions as to what he regards as being the *real* content of the community-based curriculum; or, whether all that he is claiming is that learning will be enhanced through the motivational effects of involving a child in learning which entails his interaction with his environment. If the first, then all we have is a restatement of the mainstream curriculum which is so general that it is hard to see how it can provide the facilitating body of knowledge that will achieve the radical aims it is intended to achieve. If the second, then this begs the question as to whether such content will provide motivational answers. Can it be claimed that if the school curriculum reflects the community in as many respects as possible then that curriculum will be intrinsically of more interest and concern – will be more relevant – to inner-city children?

In point of fact, a counter claim could be advanced, that the children, having to cope with this demanding environment outside school with all the family pressures it exerts, may respond more positively to a curriculum which does not reflect or include this environment, at least to the extent that the community-based curriculum seeks to include it. It may be so: there appears to be little if any evidence for either viewpoint. Emanz (1968) in a small-scale study concluded that his group of American inner-city elementary school children preferred folk tales and stories to reading material which was based on life in the inner city. Whatever Midwinter may claim, it can only be supposition until more is known of the effects resulting from the child–environment interaction where this is present in the curriculum of inner-city schools.

This developmental disjunction therefore is a serious defect in Midwinter's thinking about the curriculum. The second problem goes deeper. There is a well-founded body of conclusions about the development of children which have educational implications. The developmental map of the junior-school-age range, for example, would need to be taken account of, whatever the orientation of the curriculum or the socioeconomic condition of the children. Midwinter's reinterpretation of history, geography, science and religious education within the terms of reference of a claimed community-orientated curriculum are not distinctive of that curriculum. They are general statements about these subject areas, part of which attempts to define what will be possible in learning and teaching, considering the general developmental levels of children in the junior-school-age range. So, has Midwinter formulated the bases for a community-orientated curriculum, or has he done no more than reiterate the general developmental preconditions and pre-requisites for studying these subject areas? His wording would translate equally to inner-city schools, suburban schools, rural schools or commuter-belt schools, since it is children, and not a curriculum that he is talking about.

It seems that little progress has been made in identifying the possible content and procedures for a community-based curriculum. All that exists is a statement of its long-term aims, a framework, and claims about the need for it to be a relevant educational experience for inner-city children, whatever this means. What seems to be enmeshing the notion as Midwinter and Halsey see it is the myth of relevancy, as it may be termed, and the dogma which follows from it: that the only legitimate means of learning for inner-city children will be through their exposure to as many facets as possible of their own environment, working on the assumption that children just must see its relevance as being the legitimate content for their education. Given its Utopian perspectives, the political-social implications of this concept of education cannot be ignored. Children are being prepared to come to terms with living in an educational priority area, or in the inner city. As to whether they are at the same time being prepared to negotiate successfully with those agencies retaining political and economic power in order to improve the quality of life in these areas remains a further question. It is fair to separate these two possible functions in the light of the discussion so far. This is education as social engineering, not an education which has social engineering as one of its functions.

One test which may be applied is how schools perceive this as a claimed legitimate view of education. An important aim discussed by Midwinter (1972b) which he sees as part of the enabling process is that of changing teachers' attitudes so that they will become receptive to a community-based curriculum. The intention is that they would see its relevance for inner-city children. He indicates that the teachers his project team were working with in Liverpool were concerned that basic skills in reading, writing and computation would not be neglected in the project, and he suggests that 'The teachers' conventional support of certain established planks may have to be lessened as they endeavour to conduct an objective examination of the issues facing people today in the city areas'.

Again there is the problem of relevance: of what Midwinter and the Liverpool teachers respectively saw as being relevant to the children's education, and the conflicting values underlying different interpretations of need.

In conclusion, it is argued that any education which is as narrowly conceived as the Midwinter-Halsey conception of community education runs the danger of disadvantaging children rather than widening their educational perspectives. There is a considerable gap here between the intended end-results of the process, and what the product is likely to be. The 'downtown curriculum for downtown children' comment may on the face of it seem unjustified when the aims of this concept of education are considered, but questions have to be asked as to whether the strategies planned are likely to achieve these.

Much of the discussion in this chapter has taken the form of an analysis of the Midwinter-Halsey notion of community education as representing the most ambitious attempt so far to formulate a cogent radical interpretation of an educational alternative for the inner city. But, in practice, it never quite gets clear of its origins, in the Plowden Committee's notion of community education, which in turn has its roots in a compensatory viewpoint of urban education. It will be useful at this stage to turn to one aspect of a parallel project so as to examine some of the issues which have been identified here in a more specific context.

Chapter 5

The Deptford project

This project in many ways typifies the aims of the EPA action research programmes. In particular, it is a good illustration of the attempt to reinterpret traditional subjects and skills by changing their context, in order both to enhance learning and generate social awareness. The environmental studies component of the programme is of particular interest here. It is valuable as a case study since it encapsulates the central and unresolved question which inheres in the Plowden Committee's recommendations for educational provision in the priority areas: whether the educational experience should predominantly be compensatory in style, or have a strong community education and social engineering focus. It is precisely this confusion which has led to the claim made here, that community education as such has no convincing identity and is another expression of the compensatory viewpoint. What remains to be explored is whether a community-based curriculum could provide a basis for a style of community education which would be a positive extension of the compensatory view, if it cannot be an alternative to it. Or, failing this, what might be retrieved from different interpretations of the notion, and where might this be placed in a school curriculum.

The Deptford project has been examined in detail by Barnes (1975) in Volume 3 of the *Educational Priority* series of reports. In his role of evaluator he was particularly concerned with the core area of activity of the project – or at least, its most spectacular and ambitious enterprise – which was the environmental studies scheme. It is in this scheme that a micro-view of the whole EPA action research rationale in its radical form can be seen.

It was very much a field trial as befits an action research setting, designed to investigate the potential of this sort of scheme in inner-city schools. There were two problems which made evaluation difficult: firstly, there was no general scheme having a common framework, but one for each class of children participating under in many cases very different conditions. Secondly, there was a compromise over objectives. These emerged as formulations of general intent with which all of those participating would agree. Thus, the scheme, rather than establishing a set of objectives, which were designed to bring about planned learning outcomes, moved towards a consensus position on how to proceed. So, in rather an *ad hoc* way, a process view of the environmental studies scheme emerged, instead of the stipulated objectives, means–ends model which was first envisaged.

But while such an interpretation would seem to be an appropriate way of managing what was a complex and essentially diffuse project, this particular mode of operating was never made explicit as a mode by its participants. In practice, there was no clearly delineated operational model. This caused problems for evaluation. It was decided for example, that evaluation would proceed on the presupposition that the scheme was homogeneous rather than accepting and taking account of the diversity within it. The reason for this was that it was thought that detailed class by class evaluation would be seen by the teachers as a threat to their professional role, and that it might disrupt 'the delicate coalition of interests', as Barnes puts it.

In fact the confusion caused by what emerged as a general list of educational expectations, as distinct from agreed objectives, made for crucial problems both of evaluation and of credibility in the teachers' eyes, because the scheme lacked a recognisable frame of reference.

Eventually, a set of seven general objectives was agreed upon. They included improvements in pupils' and teachers' attitudes and motivation; an increase in parental involvement; and the development of a programme which would be an environmental study in its own right, and which would also permeate other school learning activities. The project director, Charles Betty, claimed that the scheme succeeded in all these areas, but Barnes is more sceptical. He has three reservations. Firstly, little emphasis was placed on the improvement of children's cognitive skills, even though one of the objects of the programme was to improve learning, especially in skills-based classroom work. Secondly, the list of objectives, which was more in the nature of a list of intentions as has been discussed, indicated other hoped-for results. The 'objectives' as they were stated, seemed to be little more than a list of aspirations, which it was hoped the environmental study would facilitate. There was no close match between the conception of the environmental studies scheme and what counted amongst teachers and the project team as objectives which the scheme would realise. Thirdly, the objectives in the form they took did not readily lend themselves either to formative or summative evaluation, but were there to provide guidance as to how the study should proceed. The problem, both of evaluation and operation was compounded by the fact that they proved ineffective as guidelines because they were not grounded in the scheme itself. They appeared to reside in some educational limbo, as aspirations in the minds of those concerned, but not located sufficiently securely in the pedagogical vehicle through which it was intended that these aspirations would be realised. The problem then was inherent in the organisation of the scheme itself, and was more fundamental than simply emphasising means and assuming ends.

It is likely that this is a characteristic of the form of action research adopted by the EPA projects, given their limited time span and funding. The focus is likely to be fixed on mounting programmes which will achieve, or appear to achieve, preconceived or desired outcomes, according to given terms of reference as to what ought to characterise education in the inner city. The whole issue of the community-based curriculum is a focal point here, and in view of its position in the social-educational structure of community education, perhaps it is not surprising that it has not received a great amount of close, critical scrutiny from protagonists. Van der Eyken's (1974) comment that 'The idea of the "community school" with its focus on a local, relevant curriculum, related to its environment will undoubtedly lead to further development' is optimistic, considered against the developing ideology of community education.

In this sort of climate, the evaluation of objectives can be neglected in the need to produce desired results. It raises, moreover, the general question of what kind of curriculum design will be most suitable. Assuming it were possible to formulate agreed goals, there are doubts as to whether a behavioural objectives curriculum model is suited to action research projects of the EPA type, given their complexity, short existence, and the problem of establishing what is in fact their rationale. Likewise, the short-term format suggests that if a model which emphasised processes as against objectives were to be adopted, the time constraints would impede the emergence of any reliable conclusions as to how further developments might proceed. This is the dilemma which beset the Deptford project, and which is vividly portrayed in the environmental studies programme. There was an uneasy relationship between designing and implementing the scheme and establishing the means of evaluating it.

This particular programme, then, lacked a rationale in the shape of publically arrived-at principles, and it is difficult to see how this might have been achieved considering the circumstances. As Barnes comments:

'Everybody, it was assumed, "knew" what the Environmental Studies scheme was about. As it transpired, I think, the scheme was about three things, with an inevitable fourth only in the mid-distance. It was about children enjoying school. It was about providing experiences for children in urban EPA schools which a "good parent" ought to provide. It was about offering children intrinsically worthwhile experiences. And in the

distance was a further concern: for the school performance of the youngsters.' (p. 175.)

He discusses several levels of educational thinking where the purposes of the scheme could be found. They ranged from a desire that schools should do something pleasurable for their pupils, and that at a further remove, this would improve their attitudes towards school; to the contention that schools should compensate overtly for parental inadequacies by providing experiences which a competent parent would normally provide. Deprivation, here, was seen as a lack of access to the countryside, and therefore a rural studies scheme would be educationally worthwhile.

Barnes takes issue with how this was perceived. The experience was in the teachers' hands and was seen as being explicitly educational. The intentions were clear; that teachers would use the experience gained in the rural studies scheme to further children's educational development along particular paths and in other contexts. But the compensatory assumptions break down here, partly because of what seems to be a teachers' caricature of the leisure activities of middle-class families, and partly because the assumed need – an experience of the countryside – figured more in the minds of the teachers than in the children's. What did, or could, the rural studies experience mean to them? Quite simply, if parents take their children into the country, there is no necessary concomitant. It is an event in its own right.

To take this further, Barnes' claim, that while the assumption was made that the scheme would have an educational pay-off, it seems that this was never fully explicated either by the teachers, or the project team. Certainly, it is included in the list of agreed objectives or intentions, but it appears that the project team in fact envisaged the scheme mainly as a means for identifying possible principles for innovating in this particular field. So, the teachers had considerable, though generalised, educational expectations of the scheme, but the project team's view was less ambitious. Again, what is evident here is a reluctance on the part of the project team to engage in any debate with their teacher colleagues. The end result was a lack of communication of purpose paradoxically due to the efforts made by the team to involve teachers, and its reluctance to introduce any potentially contentious areas of discussion which might threaten collaboration.

Thus, the scheme was compromised at several levels; by a stock response notion of deprivation adopted by teachers, which eliminated the possibility of their mounting a parallel environmental studies scheme in the children's home environment; by the educational aspirations they invested in it; and perhaps crucially, by the unexpressed differences which existed between the teachers and the project team.

Eventually, two areas were identified where changes in children's educational behaviour might be expected. These were, improved attitudes towards learning in school; and improvements in learning skills. These were assessed. In summary, children ranked the environmental study activities as being the most liked in school, but there was no significant attitude change identified towards school learning generally, or in increased motivation to do well in school, compared with results obtained from a control group. Teacher–pupil relations grew worse in both experimental and control groups. In skills learning, there were no significant changes in performance as between the groups, but the study skills of the children involved in the scheme deteriorated compared with those of the control group.

It could be claimed, as has already been mentioned, that considering the circumstances, evaluation was a meaningless activity. But, evaluation did take the form of an assessment of those very skills which the teachers expected children to improve upon, as a result of the environmental studies scheme. Indeed, teachers insisted that in spite of the results of the evaluation, attitudes, motivation, relationships and learning had all improved. Considering the enthusiasm among teachers about the scheme, the question has to be posed as to whether they were perceiving desired rather than actual changes. The teachers' as against the evaluator's view is reinforced by Charles Betty, the project director, in an article in *The Times Educational Supplement* ('How the other half worked'; 9 May 1975). He maintains that nearly four years after the project ended, teachers were still of the opinion that the improvements they had claimed at the time had actually come about. He says:

'*I cannot imagine that they were greatly influenced by tests which did not assess what the teachers thought was implicit and explicit in the aims of the scheme. If research workers cannot place much reliance on teachers' opinions, parents' observations and the children's comments, perhaps they would accept the opinion of the ILEA inspectorate who, helped by an HMI, reported that the environmental studies scheme was in the main successful.*'

What counted as success, then, for these people, is in question. Betty's reference also, to 'implicit' and 'explicit' aims comments on what Barnes has already said about the nature of the scheme's aims, how they were arrived at, and how they were perceived by the different participants.

A further aim which was mentioned in Halsey's description of the scheme was that through studying a different environment, children would be enabled to compare it with their own, to adopt a critical attitude towards their own environment, and through this, develop a sense of responsibility for it. This was not included in the list of objectives and intentions. Bearing in mind how teachers saw the role and purpose of the scheme, this perhaps is not surprising. Halsey did say that this particular aim was not emphasised, and there is no information either from what has been recorded of the scheme, or the evaluation exercise, as to whether or not this did occur.

Barnes is sceptical about the educative value of the scheme and critical of its presuppositions. He also discusses its self-fulfilling nature. He notes that the ILEA through its Schools Sub-Committee regarded the scheme as being intrinsically good, despite the fact that, arguably, its educational goals were never clearly identified. A further difficulty was that, as designed, the scheme was additional to the normal curriculum, with no indications as to what it might replace or augment. This is reflected in the confusion over objectives and guidelines, and the assumptions made by teachers about its transferability, as has been discussed. It was peripheral to what was going on in the schools. This undermined its educational potential, as it was not sufficiently closely tied to the schools' routine. On the one hand, there appear to have been few cogent attempts on the part of teachers to integrate the scheme in the normal school curriculum; on the other, teachers were involved in a large-scale cooperative exercise which did claim to have broad educational aims, which in turn had community and social implications. The scheme was ambitious and had the potential to investigate what might be involved in establishing some important principles for a community-based curriculum.

It is at this stage that the debate in the previous chapter and the questions raised can be linked to the more specific investigation carried on here in order to draw together further conclusions about community education and the community-based curriculum. As to whether any organising concepts for a possible community-based curriculum have emerged, the discussion so far suggests that in the EPA projects attempts to do this have been fragmented and have taken second place within the action research context to developing teaching–learning approaches and related content. None of this has departed in a radical way from what is the normal provision.

Behind what sometimes appears to be a radical reappraisal of education in the inner city, remains the conventional curriculum with its definition as to what counts as educability. The conclusion would seem to be that compensatory strategies are unavoidable for better or ill, in the inner city, because of the way education is organised nationally and because of its enduring rationale and goals. There is nothing to suggest that its meritocratic ethos will change either because of pressures inside or outside education. No radical alternative has emerged.

The free school movement is essentially compensatory in nature. The plea for more internal democracy highlights a debate about school students having a greater say in choice of content and school organisation, rather than the goals of schooling. There are within the conventional structure elements which are described as community education, and some schools which include this as part of their programme describe themselves as community schools. This form of community education varies in its status but compared with the academic and vocational goals of the school, it is generally low. The schools where social education courses are run are by no means seen as instruments of social engineering. Indeed, it could be claimed that the majority of them are concerned with bringing their pupils to relate to legitimised mores and goals of a society through interaction with facets of it, rather than to engender ideas about how it all might be changed.

At the same time, these forms of community education have their intrinsic value. By inference, there is the positive view which teachers hold about the educability of inner-city children, and the characteristics of inner-city life, in the radical interpretation of community education. But when comparisons are made between what there is in the form of community education, and its radical stance as espoused by Midwinter and Halsey, these comparisons amount to different concepts of education. And even then, there are doubts as to the autonomy of the radical viewpoint. As Hatch and Moylan suggest:

'*To make progress with a radical community approach, certain conditions are necessary. The school needs to be identified with a given area and take nearly all, if not all, the children from that area. This involves some curtailment of parental choice, and defining a comprehensive school as one which recruits all the children from an area rather than one with a "balanced" intake in terms of intelligence and social class. Such a recruitment policy can only be justified if accompanied by a policy of positive discrimination, such that schools which are disadvantaged in terms of facilities and intake receive priority in the allocation of resources.*' (p. 222.)

It is suggested here that this has as much or more to say about how children might be compensated educationally in an inner city area, rather than laying down preconditions for radical community education. The compensatory experience, as a precondition for a community education approach, which Hatch and Moylan seem to be advocating, presents problems of linkage, which have been discussed.

There are many disparate elements and the question remains as to whether these can be resolved in trying to establish a set of concepts which could be used to develop an education for the inner-city child which could truly be described as being relevant to his educational needs. And an overriding consideration is whether this can be, or should be, different from that experienced by children in more favoured areas socially and environmentally. The problem focuses upon the linkage between equality in education, however this is interpreted, and how educability is perceived. If compensatory strategies are unavoidable, then the compensatory view must be shed. A way of doing this is to change its location. Up till now it has been seen in terms of the educational mainstream and its requirements and the possibility of changing children to such an extent academically, that they will be able to compete with others more favoured, at the pointed end of the meritocracy pyramid. If compensatory education was for instance seen as being part of a common education, there is the possibility of re-interpreting it positively. This is a major consideration in the next chapter, where the possibilities presented by a common curriculum are explored, along with other attempts to formulate a relevant educational experience for inner-city children, and in which the notion, if not the substance, of community education plays an important part.

Chapter 6

The future of community education

Towards the end of the last chapter, it was suggested that the compensatory view of schooling was unavoidable in the absence of clear guidelines or statements about a possible educational experience which stemmed from a community-based curriculum. The question therefore is, how can the compensatory notion shed its perjorative associations which it has acquired through its interpretation of educability? Allied with this is the possibility of extracting those elements of community education which seem realisable in an inner-city setting, and which at the same time make a contribution to the general education of inner-city children. The inference here is that the radical statement of community education would contribute by virtue of the positive views inherent in it about the nature of educability, the importance of parental involvement in schooling, and the value it ascribes to the inner-city environment as a valid source of learning experiences. But, the social engineering aim, where it is made explicit, would be shed.

The charge might be made, that this represents such an emasculation of the radical interpretation of community education that the 'mainstream' moderate view of it might as well be adopted. But, as has already been discussed, this is so inadequate as a medium for education that it presents more problems than advantages. In fact, it need not impinge on what might be seen by parents and teachers and children as the legitimate business of the school. Against the possible charge of emasculation can be brought the counter-charge, that such an education, even if it were possible to establish it with a full-blown community curriculum geared to the organising principle of constructive discontent, would be so narrow an experience that it would be educationally self-defeating. It is near-fantasy to believe that the products of such an education could develop the skills, knowledge, perspectives, and the social maturity to meet the purveyors of power on an equal or superior footing.

There seem to be two alternatives. The dominant one is the notion of the common curriculum which has been espoused by Lawton (1969; 1973; 1975) and by White (1973). The other entails a reinterpretation of the alternative high school movement in the USA so that it might achieve parity in every sense with the mainstream of education. Farrington, Pritchard and Raynor pose this question in their survey of the Parkway Program, and they express surprise that similar experimental schools have not been established here. Both of these possibilities will be examined in an attempt to come to some conclusions about the problematic notion of relevance as it applies to inner-city education.

The common curriculum

The common curriculum notion in many ways shares the egalitarian rationale of those educationalists concerned with education in the inner city, and cogent statements are emerging about its possible theoretical foundations and how these might be put to work. There are many similarities and differences. Both the radical community education view and that of the common curriculum imply changes in curriculum content, teaching approaches, and, perhaps most crucial of all, teachers' attitudes about the nature of educability. But while the community curriculum repudiates the traditional goals of schooling, except as required instruments for achieving longer-term ends, the common curriculum largely retains these. The notion of the common curriculum has reached a higher level of articulation than that of the community-based curriculum; it has been concerned with epistemological questions, with school organisation, and certain views about the pedagogy involved are emerging. Contrasted with this, the community-based curriculum and the radical view of community education founded on it has produced statements about its theoretical position only, and these at a fairly general and embryonic level. Also, it has failed to reconcile its social engineering with its educative function, and it is not enough merely to conflate the two. If this is done, the charge of indoctrination can be made, and the whole enterprise ruled out on ethical grounds as constituting education.

The initial question which will be explored here is whether the idea of a common curriculum is a more practicable one than that of a community-based curriculum. Also to what extent, if any, might they be unified or made to complement each other. Further to this is the consideration of how compensatory strategies may be used in a re-cast form. This might involve, for instance, jettisoning the term 'compensatory' with its judgemental overtones.

Both notions begin from egalitarian stances. Lawton (1973; 1975) claims that common schools, by which he means fully comprehensive secondary schools, must, if they are to be credible, transmit a common culture, and the means for individual development will be provided for in this. If this is not done, then any discussion of equality in education is meaningless. In summarising his position, Lawton says:

'*The three most important factors in this reformed educational process are: a worthwhile and relevant curriculum; the availability of carefully planned materials and methods suited to a wide range of abilities and interests; and perhaps most important of all, teachers who believe that this kind of curriculum for all pupils is desirable and possible.*' (p. 98.)

A preliminary comment is that this interpretation of a common curriculum answers the demands made by society of its education system in much the same way that traditionally organised secondary education does. It shares the same goals, such as the encouragement of academic excellence; the development of cognitive and social skills and insights valued by society, and it prepares pupils vocationally and for further education.

Where it differs from radical community education is in its interpretation of equality and what this entails at the practical level. It does not anticipate massive changes in the political structure, nor is it a preparation for this end. It seeks to extend equality of opportunity by erecting a fully comprehensive education system having a common curriculum. Broadly, the notion encapsulates a flat equalitarian view, a commonality of educational experience which will increase the amount of equality within the social and economic parameters of today's society, by treating people in much the same way. The community-based curriculum, on the other hand, subscribes to a distributive justice view of equality, where the differences rather than the similarities between children become dominant. This amounts to children experiencing an education which stems from their distinctive social, and at a further remove, political, needs, as these are defined by advocates of community education. Such an education will prepare them to obtain more equality through an acquired ability to change the political and social structure. The formulation of the common culture curriculum has a developing theoretical rationale and clear practical applications; despite the interests expressed in its possibilities by groups outside education, it is essentially an educators' view of education. The radical community education view is less secure theoretically, and has no clear practical application. Its perspectives are essentially political and economic.

This contrast implies that the common curriculum notion has inherent advantages. They can be seen in such features as relative coherence, practicability, and in its potential for replacing what counts as the mainstream. Lawton and White are in no doubt about the inadequacies of present curriculum content, especially at the secondary level, and they see a common curriculum as its replacement. Midwinter and Halsey would seek to provide an alternative which is both less ambitious, and less likely to be taken seriously by the educational decision makers, since it presents no threat to the *status quo*, and could readily be diminished, or defused, if it was confined to designated inner-city areas such as exist already in the form of educational priority areas.

In this respect, Lawton makes a similar point to that of Merson and Campbell's, that the radical community education view of curriculum relevance could result in rendering children educationally disadvantaged, and this is a conclusion which has been reached here also. He questions whether the community-based curriculum can include what he considers to be important questions about the nature of knowledge, for example. In an earlier study (1973) he poses three questions which might be applied to possible curriculum content, given his view of the curriculum, that it is a selection from the culture of a society. These are:

1. Is it worthwhile? (i.e., in the sense that there are certain aspects of education which are permanent and which express human qualities, ideas and values which a society values sufficiently highly that it desires to pass these on to the next generation.)
2. Is it relevant? (That is, to people living in this society now.)
3. What is the best way of organising agreed content for efficient learning? (Assuming that resources are reasonable rather than ideal.)

His approach to the content of such a curriculum is through educational disciplines, and he concludes that there are six such elements in a common culture curriculum: mathematics, the physical and biological sciences, humanities and social sciences (including history, geography, classical studies, social studies, literature, film and television, and religious studies) the expressive and creative arts, moral education, and interdisciplinary studies. Because there are various conflicting views about the disciplines, he would not claim that this is a definitive list, but he makes the general point that these differ from traditional school subjects because of their logical coherence and, hence, their relevance to contexts outside the purely educational. The claim made by Hirst (1965) is virtually the same: that school subjects are arbitrary divisions between bodies of knowledge, lacking inner coherence, and having meaning only in an educational setting.

There are problems besetting discipline-based curricula. On the face of it, a statement of disciplines closely resembles a list of the traditional academic subjects, and critics such as Young (1971), Keddie (1971), and Esland (1971) have asserted that the Hirst formulation, which would seem to be close to Lawton's, is no more than a reiteration of the traditional subject areas. These are not seen as being problematic and thereby open to enquiry and criticism but are accepted as being immutable. Despite the defects in their critique, pointed out for instance by Pring (1972), there remains the danger that such a curriculum could become as atrophied and institution-bound as the traditional subjects-based curriculum has become in Lawton's view – and this in spite of his claim that as a society changes, so will a common culture curriculum reflect such change.

The problem here lies in what constitutes a culture. Is it a matter of procedures, which surely do change but so imperceptibly that it might be difficult if not impossible for a curriculum to reflect this? Or is a culture to be seen more in terms of its products? Lawton's view of culture is not closely defined, and this makes for problems in the area of curriculum change. There is a difference between modifications made to a given curriculum pattern, which in essence remains unchanged, even though it no longer fully represents societal changes; and the perception of cultural changes which result in dissatisfaction with what is being taught because it is obsolete and therefore lacks relevance. Paradoxically, a common curriculum could prove to be more resistant to change than the piecemeal type of curriculum operating today. It is a short step from a common culture curriculum to a sabre-tooth curriculum; a piecemeal state of affairs allows innovations to varying extents, whereas a common curriculum in practice could become monolithic.

Furthermore, a common curriculum both draws upon the culture of a society, and is imposed on that society through its education service. The administrative implications suggest centralised control, and a danger here is the one discussed earlier in the context of official notions of deprivation applied to inner-city areas – that assumptions could be made about a general uniformity of educational need as a society sees this through its educators. This in turn could have the result that legitimate local needs so far as people in certain sub-cultures are concerned, might be ignored, or simply not perceived as special needs.

This in turn raises questions about the criteria for deciding worth-whileness. The rationale of the common curriculum is that all children will benefit from the selection made from the culture. Strong arguments have been advanced for a selection to be made on an educational disciplines basis, but other interpretations are possible, and could be made. There is for example the range and types of curriculum offerings made by the American alternative high schools as discussed here. Also, who makes the selection? The concept, it has been suggested is an educators' concept, but ideological factors, to do with economic viability, regeneration and growth, political stability, and pressures to retain as far as possible the *status quo* in schools, are likely to influence the choice made or actually determine it, whoever is making the choice.

Again, certain areas of study to do with literacy and numeracy virtually choose themselves, but what is to accompany them could be a matter for contention.

The possible conflict between different sectional interests in choosing a curriculum raises questions about the achievement of its main educational aims, and especially that of increasing the amount of equality. If the curriculum is chosen on a strongly instrumental basis, for example, so as to serve economic needs more directly, then this could introduce a greater selectivity in schooling than exists now, with a consequent strengthening of the meritocratic nature of education. Equality would hardly be served by this. Also, in the concern to serve economic, or social, interests, much that is of intrinsic educational value could be left out. Adjusting teaching methods, organisation and content might well result in improved learning, and higher achievement in examinations, but these do not in themselves comment on what is being taught. Peters' (1966) discussion of equality is relevant here. He is concerned with both the flat equalitarian and the distributive justice viewpoints. His conclusion is that the best that any education system by itself can do is to minimise actual inequalities. The real questions, to do with permissible amounts of opportunity lie outside the dispensation of the education system. This might also apply to how 'common' is defined.

In summary, such reservations about the potential of a common curriculum to increase equality bear on questions of worthwhileness and how this might differently be perceived by different interests; and how flexible the curriculum can be in recognising special and specific needs and being able to satisfy these. Commonality does not necessarily mean uniformity, but a crude interpretation might indicate this.

The contribution from community education

In order to consider what might be retrieved from community education, it is necessary to look at its unexpressed rationale, rather than its polemical social engineering statements of intent. The desire to promote a community consciousness is difficult to unravel. There are strong emotive forces behind this which are concerned with the conditions of material deprivation, the various dimensions and manifestations of inequality, wastage of ability, and a seeming desire on the part of many project workers to identify with people in the inner city, almost out of a sense of reparation. Perhaps a characteristic here is the attitude of many educationalists and social workers, for instance, of working-class origins, who succeeded educationally, and who feel an obligation to plough back their educational profits. The other side of the coin of course, are those who use their success as an exit visa. The first view-point is expressed in a wide continuum of attitudes and activities. There is the missionary do-gooding role of some teachers; at another remove, there is the desire to seek out like talent and sponsor it. And at an extreme, there is the belief in political and economic goals of a frankly Utopian kind.

None of this is intended to denigrate. But it does help to pinpoint the uneasy meshing of emotional concern and identification with the inner-city malaise, and planned attempts to cure it. In an unexpressed and indeed unrealised way, this acknowledges the meritocratic functioning and organisation of English education. The object, both of explicit social engineering goals, and the sponsoring of talent can equally be about social and economic changes which will place the quality of living and the culture of the inner city on a level with areas more favoured environmentally and socially. Cultural disadvantage is a label tacitly accepted by community educationalists, and cultural parity is their aim. One of the strengths of the common curriculum notion which has not been articulated so far, is that it accepts the meritocratic ethos, of the selective function of education through success and failure in public examinations. In fact it is arguable that the apparatus for such selection is so deeply imbedded in all education systems in developed countries that without it, such systems would lose their *raison d'être*. The function of an education system is to prepare individuals for life in a society by involving them in a monitored and scaled-down model of life in that society.

How then can community education be considered as a valid and relevant educational experience? However imperfect and incomplete its rationale might be, its main organising principle includes a positive view of the educational potential of the inner city child, and ways in which this might be realised. The intention, to identify and ameliorate deficiencies in local conditions is a linked and equally valuable general proposition. The aim of sensitising children to the conditions of their material and cultural environment so as to enable them to compare it critically with other environments has, it is contended here, a general application. It is not part and parcel of urban education alone. It should be included in the education of all children, whatever their living conditions and social environment. It has much to do with achieving self-knowledge, and a sense of personal location.

Furthermore, an awareness of community is by no means a pre-condition for this. It is sufficient that children come to an understanding of the day-to-day workings of their neighbourhood; why certain values, which are not always expressed, govern behaviour in it; and what are the beliefs and traditions implied in these. This does not add up to a sense of community. It describes an awareness which can be fostered and helped to crystallise in schools, of life for an individual in a certain place, at a certain time in history; why and how conditions came about; what they are; and whether they are changing in any marked way. What is central here is that this has more to do with a sense of self-awareness developing, than with a claimed sense of community responsibility. The point becomes more compelling if such an awareness is seen as a precondition for community awareness. In point of fact, the radical interpretation of community education can be stood on its head, and its facilitating notion, of constructive discontent, reinforces this: that the whole view in reality has more to say about achieving self-awareness than about developing a sense of community responsibility. The move must be from the personal to the social.

This discussion, then, has everything to do with recognising the primacy of the individual in an educational process, and of his initiation into areas of knowledge which will help him towards developing perspectives about himself and his life. Whether or not these take a sociopolitical shape later is a further question. So, these elements of community education are legitimate inclusions in a general education experience. By inference, they underline further the serious defects and deficiencies in the claim made by community educationalists: that the radical interpretation is a viable alternative to the mainstream. There are no educational solutions for the conditions having the degree of material and emotional deprivation which are encountered in many inner-city areas, and these are the places where, according to the research by Keller a sense of community in a limited, street by street way can be seen to exist. Self-protective and inward-looking attitudes which both distrust the outside world and repudiate, if it is understood, the possibility of change, are factors here. To apply a community-centred notion of education in these conditions would at best be treating symptoms rather than causes. At worst, no form of education whatever its orientation will make an impression on 'the psychological meaning of poverty'.

This invokes a point made in the previous chapter, that part of a relevant education for the EPA and the inner city will be compensatory in nature. Much can be said in support for this. It satisfies the distributive justice view, in that specific educational needs would be considered within a framework of general education. In the first two chapters, the compensatory standpoint was criticised and the conclusion was, that by itself, it is inherently unsuited to meeting educational needs because of its negative view of inner-city children, as being educational deficit systems. The rejoinder can be made that in some respects they are. But unless the notion has within it the potential for developing a positive view of educability, it is self-defeating.

What seems to be lacking here is an appreciation of the affective side of learning and teaching. The efforts made in the Liverpool and Deptford projects to modify teachers' attitudes and expectations emerged as one of the main conclusions drawn by Halsey about the EPA projects' attempt to identify guidelines for urban education. It was an attempt to get teachers to develop new ideas about the nature of educability, linked with acceptance of a modified curriculum. Whatever conclusions may be drawn about the way this was seen through the preconceptions in the projects, the enterprise itself has value. The possibility of developing in children a self-awareness which might project so that the personal informs the social has everything to do with reconciling the cognitive with the affective in education. This is a neglected area in English schools; the cognitive achieves ascendancy from the time usually during the infant school, when the child has reached a level of expertise in reading and computation which makes independent learning and the measurement of his achievements possible. At the level of values, when statements of educational aims are examined, there is often an uneasy juxtaposition between what can be called social aims – to do with economic viability in the main – and those which express self-development. The Plowden Committee's discussion of the aims of primary education is a good example; so too is the discussion of the middle years of schooling in Schools Council Working Paper 42 (1972).

So far as school learning is concerned, Fantini and Weinstein (1968) argue for what they claim would be a reversal of the normal order, in their discussion of the nature of disadvantage and its educational remedies. In their view the cognitive should serve the affective in learning. They have developed an instructional model from which both learning and teaching strategies and principles for designing a curriculum could be derived. Although the cognitive and the affective are interdependent, the affective is dominant. They see this as being crucial to children developing what they describe as educational concerns, which must be distinguished from interests. Concerns have to do with areas of learning which have a strong personal reference, which in turn provoke inner drives towards resolution which is achieved through learning. Interests, by comparison, are more superficial; while they might reflect concerns, they are by nature less heavily charged with the kind of personal unease which denotes what a child needs to know.

The curriculum model which derives from this contrasts the direct experiences of children with the assertion that these are neglected in the classroom through the essentially verbal means by which teaching is conducted:

'*A curriculum for the disadvantaged must begin as closely as possible to the pupils' direct experience; without such an approach, the abstract cannot be attained. By definition,* to abstract *means* to represent *something that is real, and the basis for abstraction must be based on the concrete reality of the individual to have any meaning for him. Too often teachers assume that the words they use are related to the child's world, when, in truth, they have little or no relationship to him. Many problems in disadvantaged schools stem from this discrepancy. The cardinal rule could be "Experience first; we'll talk later".'* (p. 347.)

The curriculum should move from being symbolistic to being experiential; in its content, from being remote to being immediate; from concern with 'what' to the consideration of 'why'. What is important here is that their thinking goes a long way towards identifying a mode of educating in which compensatory strategies could be used, detached from the notion of compensatory education, as part of a relevant experience for inner-city children. It is important also to point out that their theoretical framework both derives from and has been refined further by practical experience of teaching in urban schools over a long period. Also, if anything, it is a more radical answer than that of the radical interpretation of community education. Their discussion of why the curriculum should move from being academic to being a participating curriculum includes, for example, possible active involvement in Civil Rights demonstrations by Negro children. What is being aimed at is the development of a positive self-concept through a school experience which includes social action if this is needed. They consider how the Bruner notion of the spiral curriculum could be used as a frame of reference which would begin in the elementary school and continue into high school. Similarly, when they claim that the curriculum should become reality-orientated and move away from being academic, they maintain that such a curriculum must help children answer two key questions: how has society been a major contributing factor to the more negative conditions of all the people in the country, and to certain groups of people in particular? How have these social factors led to ways in which we define ourselves as individuals? They comment: 'These questions take on special significance when considered in relation to the Negro child.'

But clearly, such a curriculum has a wider application. This can be seen in their treatment of educational goals which in summary attempts to integrate the development of self-identity and of personal concerns, the identification and fostering of gifts and talents, and the provision for basic skills learning. These do not represent different goals; rather, they are a more refined statement of the traditional goals of schooling, underpinned by a recognised interdependence of the cognitive and the affective in learning. This curriculum-centred interpretation suggests a pedagogical basis for a common curriculum which has been lacking till now.

Although it would appear that there are no direct connections between Fantini and Weinstein's work and that of the alternative high schools, both ethos share many values. The practical difference of course is that Fantini and Weinstein's thinking has yet to be spelt out in terms of actual school programmes, though elements of it can be found in the work of the alternative schools.

The alternative high schools: problems and possibilities

It remains, then, to consider whether the experiments with alternative high schools in the USA in particular could be reinterpreted so that a relevant urban education might be developed from these; relevant both in the sense of providing those conditions and experiences which will make sense to the inner-city child, and achieve parity with the educational mainstream. Farrington, Pritchard, and Raynor in their Parkway study make what seem to be equivocal comments as to the future development of alternatives. On the one hand, they see Parkway and similar experiments as providing models which have implications for urban education in general. They express surprise that there has not been the same scale of experimentation in this country. On the other hand, they suggest that Parkway represents a model of schooling with universal applications:

'*It implies a widening of the concept of a school and the present boundaries of the curriculum, and the roles of both student and teacher. Parkway challenges the traditional concept of a school, because it is open to the community and to new ideas, and it encourages openness between students, teachers, parents, and the community. Parkway represents a movement towards different types of learning situations in which a self-determined curriculum is one of the principle features. . . . Parkway challenges the traditional role of the student as a passive receiver of learning.*' (p. 198.)

Although Parkway and the others were born out of crisis and represent attempts at 'education in community' as Newmann and Oliver would describe it, they are exemplifiers of a form of general education. In this, they have been somewhat compromised by the label 'alternative', as a form which operates alongside the conventional. They are alternative in their expressing of a different educational philosophy. Whereas the common curriculum reorders the piecemeal curriculum of the mainstream – and because it is essentially conservative, is a stronger candidate for adoption – the example of the alternative schools rejects the mainstream curriculum and adopts a view of content which is student-determined. But when this is considered more closely, the mainstream is not as far removed as the alternative philosophy might indicate. The same basic skills, of literacy in particular, are needed, perhaps more acutely in the curriculum offerings. The retention of high-school graduation, although required by the boards of education, does not seem to have resulted in any major modification of the curriculum rationale. Students are enabled to proceed on to higher forms of education and into jobs with much the same sorts of expertise as that of their contemporaries in conventional schools.

It has been suggested earlier here that such experiments might represent the first phase of a radical reappraisal of education, but that in the process, they will lose their identity as features from their programmes are assimilated by the mainstream. Another possibility lies in the kind of threat they level at the conventional which can also be attributed to the radical view of community education here: if they were seen as threatening, the expedient thing to do would be to allow them the status of urban high schools, only, with a neighbourhood intake. This serves to point out two aspects from which they both derive strength and are vulnerable: in their experimental nature, and in their balanced ethnic and geographical intake. But, they are curriculum-based institutions in the Fantini and Weinstein sense; they also go some way towards meeting the assertion that the cognitive must serve the affective, in exploring and developing students' concerns in education.

Their vulnerability cannot be denied, and in view of this and the relative strength of the common curriculum notion, what needs to be explored is the possibility of incorporating a more affective orientation of learning and teaching in a common curriculum. The problematic situation of compensatory strategies needs also to be clarified. Another question which requires answering is, how flexible might a common curriculum view be, in including content which fulfils local educational needs?

A common education

It is important to recognise that such a curriculum, if it is to be truly common and representative of the culture, should apply to the whole statutory age range of schooling. Most of the recent work on the common curriculum has been focused on the secondary school, which is a serious weakness in the whole notion of commonality. The roots of a common secondary school curriculum will need to be established in the primary school.

This assumes that the primary–secondary division is retained, whether it occurs at 11 + or within a first-middle-upper-schools type of organisation, with transfer at 12 or 13 years. At any rate, the most productive approach entails considering the 5 to 16 years age range from a general developmental viewpoint, bearing in mind that a growing body of research is available about children's development. This can be applied to educational contexts, and to the formulating of a curriculum.

An advantage in being obliged to consider the whole age range is that it puts the disciplines into perspective, if the curriculum is to be conceived of in terms of disciplines. They need not be seen as being distinctive of secondary education exclusively, with integrated, activity-centred and basic skills learning characterising primary education. A possible sequence of educational experience might be as follows: an introduction to schooling through structured and guided play with other children; the introduction and acquisition of basic skills in language and mathematics, especially computation, as well as the social skills of cooperating and sharing. Two senses of skills is suggested: those instrumental in the short term, such as basic computation, reading, writing, being able to communicate verbally; and higher-order or long-term skills such as being able to identify and discuss a problem whether general, personal, or task-orientated, in a rational way; of being able to recapitulate the series of moves by which a problem was solved and its solution justified. Also, having the sensitivity towards language to be able to develop through the ability to discuss and listen, long-standing concerns, reinforced through being made aware of individual potential for action.

Following this, the possibility of introducing children to learning which will help them to develop further as persons should be established in several related but discrete areas of consciousness. Chief among these would be the imaginative; the cognitive; the social and emotional; and the aesthetic. These areas of consciousness will help children to relate what they know of their surroundings at different levels, beginning with the physical, and what they might begin to know about themselves. This stage in the sequence is seen as the point where consolidation of skills learned, and the first results of learning based on these and recognisable to the children will occur. The orientation is strongly personal and affective – it has much to do with horizon broadening, seen as inner horizons – and the characteristic learning outcomes will be stamped with this sense of emerging personalities. Areas of consciousness have been mentioned. These will be linked with areas of activity: the term is used because it refers neither to subjects or 'activities'. These will include language investigation in several forms; mathematics; dance; music; physical education; games; and art and craft.

Additionally, a form of social studies might be introduced which will begin to look at human behaviour and development. It will investigate what is distinctively human, but at this point, a general biological focus might be more suited to what are likely to be younger children. The organising notion for this area of activity would be the multiplicity of differences which exist within the one species, in physical, social, ethnic, religious and ethical terms.

At this stage, study of the neighbourhood would be indirect; the neighbourhood would be a source for school learning according to what would be appropriate in the areas of activity mentioned, but not at this stage in a local studies context. In order to facilitate and develop a sense of individuality, and with this, a sense of personal possibilities, the school would try to develop in the child's thinking a notion of 'in school' contrasted with a notion of 'out of school'. The bridge between these would take the form of active parental participation both in and out of school, in the child's learning. This notion of role and place of course exists, but whereas schools tend to try to blur the distinction, the argument here is that it should be made more explicit. The intention is that it would have the effect of reinforcing a child's sense of role in the two contexts, while retaining a security-giving link through the participation of parents in the learning process.

This anticipates the next part of the sequence, where there is a growing realisation of individuality. A more individualised and broader programme can be embarked upon compared with the consciously limited experience so far offered. This would include a large proportion of enquiry-centred work. By now, much can assumed to have been consolidated in basic skills, skills related to defining and working on a problem, and a sufficient body of knowledge acquired for the investigation of personal interests. Core elements such as language, mathematics, and the human development-social studies component would continue. Individual and small group topic enquiries would proceed according to the following guidelines: that they are the means of introducing historical, geographical, aesthetic, and scientific material for the future differentiation of these into separate disciplines or areas of study; and that they further the spiral development pattern implicit in this sequence.

The next part differs from the last two, in that they emphasised learning which had a strong personal reference. Certain assumptions can be made about the children. They will have reached at least the edge of a human developmental plateau cognitively; personally and emotionally, many will be entering a pre-adult phase, shown in their physical maturity and a growing sense of role and of self-consciousness. A strict Piagetian interpretation here is not intended. Rather, they will have gained the maturity to discuss matters of concern to themselves as social beings; their previous educational experience allied with other more structured learning experiences will have initiated them into an understanding of the importance of establishing sequences of activities to achieve ends, dividing and sharing responsibilities in group work, and the use of human and material resources.

Children at this point are able to understand something of the logical coherence of disciplines, and at the same time, can begin to develop attitudes towards music, the fine arts, television, films, and literature. In summary, the 'academic', represented in the introduction of disciplines, and the 'personal' as evinced by the kinds of perspectives mentioned earlier, would comprise the two curriculum strands. Moving from the descriptive to the prescriptive is consistent with this stage of educational and personal development. The human development studies could involve a planned enquiry into how people live and have lived, beginning with pupils' own neighbourhoods. This would include physical conditions, occupations, leisure, beliefs and neighbourhood mores, to help children become aware critically of problems, conflict, issues, and differing viewpoints about conditions and qualities of living.

The next stage developmentally would be initiation into the disciplines, whatever form these take. Lawton's selection, for instance, has cognitive and affective dimensions which are wide-ranging. Progress within such a common curriculum would be measured by considering ability, range, emergence of skills and interests; pupils would move to differently orientated curriculum patterns according to this idea of progress. For some the non-academic areas would be as important and as valuable as the academic, which would have implications for monitoring progress.

A further contribution from the community education notion might come through the emphasis placed on the possibility of personal action, allied with the neighbourhood-located studies. The kinds of perspectives which the radical view seeks to promote directly could develop indirectly, given this context.

A common culture-type curriculum for the whole age range implies two broad approaches: a European-type encyclopaedist one with central control and a uniform curriculum; or, using commonality as the basis and taking notice of local differences which would require schools and education authorities to reinterpret the core and to plan curriculum content according to perceived educational needs. The educational traditions of this country favours the second approach.

The issues which beset compensatory education would lapse; its strategies, however, would find their place in a remedial and not a compensatory setting. This distinction is important, since the first is instrumental, while the second comments on the value of a child's culture in an educational setting, which can prevent remedial measures from succeeding. What of course is important here, and in the whole structure, is that teachers will acquiesce in it: that they will perceive such an educational experience as being superior to what now exists.

This brief account of what a common curriculum including its pedagogy might look like for the statutory years of schooling, has tried to demonstrate the interdependence of the cognitive and the affective in learning and teaching, and to establish the principle that within a common curriculum there is and should be room for flexibility and reorientation if local conditions so require. There remains the problem of how much of this would be allowable. The answer here lies in part in the developmental picture of the age range which has been drawn, and the educational requirements which are assigned to it. The point has everything to do with Bernstein's assertion, that children should be introduced to the universalistic meanings of public forms of thought. As a guide for what education is, it has yet to be bettered.

Bibliography

Ashcroft, R. 'The school as a base for community development' in CERI (1973) *School and Community*, Paris, OECD.

Ball, C. and M. (1973) *Education for a Change*, Harmondsworth, Penguin.

Barnes, J. ed. (1975) Educational Priority, Volume 3. *Curriculum Innovation in London's EPAs*, London, HMSO.

Bennington, J. 'Community development' in Raynor, J. and Harden, J. ed. (1973) *Cities, Communities and the Young. Readings in Urban Education*, Volume 1. London, Routledge and Kegan Paul.

Bereiter, C. and Engelmann, S. (1966) *Teaching Disadvantaged Children in the Preschool*, New Jersey, Prentice Hall.

Bernstein, B. 'A critique of "compensatory education",' in Rubenstein D. and Stoneman, C. ed. (1970) *Education for Democracy*, Harmondsworth, Penguin.

Betty, C. 'How the other half worked' in *The Times Educational Supplement*, 9 May 1975.

Bremer, J. and Von Moschzisker, M. (1971) *The School Without Walls*, New York, Holt, Rinehart and Winston.

Central Advisory Council for Education (1967) (Plowden, B., Chairman) *Children and their Primary Schools*, London, HMSO.

Coates, K. and Silburn, R. 'Education in poverty' in Rubenstein, D. and Stoneman, C. ed. (1970) *Education for Democracy*, Harmondsworth, Penguin.

Daniel, S. and Maguire, P. (1972) *The Paint House*, Harmondsworth, Penguin.

Dearden, R. 'Instruction and learning by discovery' in Peters, R. ed. (1967) *The Concept of Education*, London, Routledge and Kegan Paul.

Dearden, R. (1968) *The Philosophy of Primary Education*, London, Routledge and Kegan Paul.

Douglas, J. (1964) *The Home and the School*, London, MacGibbon and Kee.

Emanz, R. 'What do children in the inner city like to read?' *Elementary School Journal*, December 1968.

Esland, J. 'Teaching and learning as the organisation of knowledge' in Young, M. F. D. ed. (1971) *Knowledge and Control*, London, Collier-MacMillan.

Eyken, Van der, W. 'Compensatory education in Britain: a review of research' in *London Educational Review*, Vol. 3, No. 3. Autumn, 1974, University of London Institute of Education.

Fantini, M. and Weinstein, G. (1968) *The Disadvantaged: Challenge to Education*, New York, Harper and Row.

Farrington, P., Pritchard, G., and Raynor, J. 'The Parkway Program' in Raynor, J. and Harden, J. ed. (1973) *Equality and City Schools. Readings in Urban Education*, Vol. 2, London, Routledge and Kegan Paul.

Ferguson, M. and Williams, P. 'The identification of children needing compensatory education' in (1969) *Children at Risk*. Occasional Paper 2, University College of Swansea Department of Education, Schools Council Research Project in Compensatory Education, Swansea. The Schools Council Publishing Co.

Floud, J., Halsey, A., and Martin, F. (1956) *Social Class and Educational Opportunity*, London, Heinemann.

Gumbert, E. (1971) 'The city as educator: how to be radical without even trying' in Raynor, J. and Harden, J. ed. (1973) *Equality and City Schools. Readings in Urban Education*, Vol. 2, London, Routledge and Kegan Paul.

Halsey, A., Floud, J., and Anderson, C. ed. (1961) *Education, Economy and Society*, New York, The Free Press.

Halsey, A. ed. (1972) Educational Priority, Volume 1, *E.P.A. Problems and Policies*, London, HMSO.

Hatch, S. and Moylan, S. (1972) 'The role of the community school' in Raynor, J. and Harden, J. ed. (1973) *Equality and City Schools. Readings in Urban Education*, Vol. 2, London, Routledge and Kegan Paul.

Hill, M. (1972) 'Community concepts and applications' in Raynor, J. and Harden, J. ed. (1973) *Cities, Communities and the Young. Readings in Urban Education*, Vol. 1, London, Routledge and Kegan Paul.

Hirst, P. 'Liberal education and the nature of knowledge' in Archambault, R. ed. (1965) *Philosophical Analysis and Education*, London, Routledge and Kegan Paul.

Hoyle, E. (1969) 'How does the curriculum change?' in Hooper, R. ed. (1971) *The Curriculum: Context, Design and Development*, Edinburgh, Oliver and Boyd.

Hoyle, E. 'The role of the change agent in educational innovation' in Walton, J. ed. (1971) *Curriculum Organisation and Design*, London, Ward Lock Educational.

Jenkins, D. and Raggatt, P. 'Alternative urban schools' in E351 Block 5. (1974) *Alternatives for Urban Schools*, Milton Keynes, Open University Press.

Jensen, A. 'How much can we boost I.Q. and scholastic achievement?' in *Harvard Educational Review*, Volume 39, No. 2, Spring, 1969.

Kagan, J. 'Inadequate evidence and illogical conclusions' in *Harvard Educational Review*, Volume 39, No. 2, Spring, 1969.

Keddie, N. 'Classroom knowledge' in Young, M. F. D. ed. (1971) *Knowledge and Control*, London, Collier-MacMillan.

Keddie, N. ed. (1973) *Tinker, Tailor . . . The Myth of Cultural Deprivation*, Introduction, Harmondsworth, Penguin.

Keller, S. (1966) 'Neighbourhood concepts in sociological perspective' in Raynor, J. and Harden, J. ed. (1973) *Cities, Communities and the Young. Readings in Urban Education*, Volume 1, London, Routledge and Kegan Paul.

Lawton, D. 'The idea of an integrated curriculum' in *Bulletin*. No. 19, Autumn Term, 1969, University of London Institute of Education.

Lawton, D. (1973) *Social Change, Educational Theory and Curriculum Planning*, London, University of London Press.

Lawton, D. (1975) *Class, Culture and the Curriculum*, London, Routledge and Kegan Paul.

MacDonald, B. and Walker, R. (1976) *Changing the Curriculum*, London, Open Books.

Mays, J. (1962) *Education and the Urban Child*, Liverpool, Liverpool University Press.

Merson, M. and Campbell, R. 'Community education: instruction for inequality' in *Education for Teaching*, No. 93, Spring, 1974. A.T.D.C.E.

Midwinter, E. (1972a) *Priority Education*, Harmondsworth, Penguin.

Midwinter, E. (1972b) *Projections*, London, Ward Lock Educational.

Midwinter, E. (1972c) *Social Environment and the Urban School*, London, Ward Lock Educational.

Midwinter, E. (1973) *Patterns of Community Education*, London, Ward Lock Educational.

Midwinter, E. (1973) 'Urban community and urban school' in Garner, N. ed. (1973) *Teaching in the Urban Community School*, London, Ward Lock.

Newmann, F. and Oliver, D. (1967) 'A proposal for education in community' in Raynor, J. and Harden, J. ed. (1973) *Equality and City Schools. Readings in Urban Education*, Vol. 2, London, Routledge and Kegan Paul.

Pahl, R. (1970) *Patterns of Urban Life*, London, Longman. (As mentioned in Hill (1972) above.)

Passow, A. and Elliott, D. 'The nature and needs of the educationally disadvantaged' in Passow, A. ed. (1968) *Developing Programs for the Educationally Disadvantaged*, New York, Teachers College Press.

Peters, R. (1966) *Ethics and Education*, London, George Allen and Unwin.

Peters, R. '"A recognisable philosophy of education." A constructive critique' in Peters, R. ed. (1969) *Perspectives on Plowden*, London, Routledge and Kegan Paul.

Pidgeon, D. (1970) *Expectation and Pupil Performance*, Slough, NFER.

Pring, R. 'Knowledge out of control' in *Education for Teaching* No. 89, Autumn 1972, ATDCE.

Schools Council Working Paper 27 (1970) '*Cross'd with Adversity*', London, Evans Bros/Methuen.

Schools Council Working Paper 42 (1972) *Education in the Middle Years*, London, Evans Bros/Methuen.

Shipman, M. (1968) *Sociology of the School*, London, Longman.

Shumsky, A. (1968) *In Search of Teaching Style*, New York, Appleton Century Crofts.

Skilbeck, M. 'Strategies of curriculum change' in Walton, J. ed. (1971) *Curriculum Organisation and Design*, London, Ward Lock Educational.

White, J. (1973) *Towards a Compulsory Curriculum*, London, Routledge and Kegan Paul.

Wiseman, S. (1964) *Education and Environment*, Manchester, Manchester University Press.

Young, M. F. D. 'An approach to the study of curricula as socially organised knowledge' in Young, M. F. D. ed. (1971) *Knowledge and Control*, London, Collier-MacMillan.

Index